SKINNY MS.
SUPERFOODS

Delicious Recipes Featuring Nature's Best Ingredients

Blackberry and Pomegranate Green Tea Smoothie *, page 22*

Skinny Ms.
SUPERFOODS

Delicious Recipes Featuring Nature's Best Ingredients

Tiffany McCauley *and* Gale Compton

QUAIL RIDGE PRESS

BRANDON, MISSISSIPPI

ISBN–13: 978–1-934193–72-3 • ISBN–10: 1-934193–72-0

Main front cover photo by Greg Campbell
Back cover photo by Gale Compton
Small cover photos and page photos by Tiffany McCauley and Gale Compton

Edited by Gwen McKee and Terresa Ray

Manufactured in the United States of America

First printing, July 2012

The nutritional data provided for this book was calculated using nutritional data soft-
ware. The combined ingredients were tabulated and divided by the number of servings.
However, using different brands of ingredients, or altering the quantities suggested in the
recipes will cause the nutritional breakdown to vary. Recipe yields may vary from those
listed regardless of brand used.

This book is not intended to be used as a medical manual. It is not intended to replace
personalized or medical council. You should always consult a doctor or nutritionist before making any drastic changes to your dietary intake.

QUAIL RIDGE PRESS
P. O. Box 123 • Brandon, MS 39043
info@quailridge.com • www.quailridge.com
www.facebook.com/cookbookladies

Dedication

For my little bear.
Thanks for being patient while Mama cooks. You're my angel.

— *Love, Mommy (Tiffany)*

I am eternally grateful for the encouragement and support shown by
Dalicia Ramey, Gene and Margaret Turner, Sarah and Al Huerta,
Wilma Tabor, Donna Morris, my happy-to-be-taste-tester Eric Turner, and
my husband Michael who is my partner in all that I do.

— *Gale*

Citrus Spinach Salad, *page 91*

Contents

Super Veggie Lasagna, *page 174*

SKINNY MS.
Introduction

Welcome to *Skinny Ms. Superfoods: Delicious Recipes Featuring Nature's Best Ingredients!* We sincerely hope the recipes presented here will help put you on the road to maximum health and fitness. Although not all food experts agree, there is ample evidence to suggest that a diet rich in superfoods can keep you at optimal health and weight, as well as help to protect you against life-threatening conditions, such as heart disease, cancer, high cholesterol, high blood pressure, and many chronic ailments.

So what are superfoods? Superfoods are whole foods that contain a high concentration of nutrients. In order for a food to be labeled a superfood, it must offer specific health benefits above and beyond its normal nutritional value. Superfoods work together with your body to nourish you at the cellular level for optimal health benefits. In general, they are whole foods that can be found among green leafy vegetables, nuts, fruits, seeds, grains, and fish. Adding superfoods to your daily menu is a smart (and yummy) way to optimize your health.

What makes a whole food a superfood? Some foods are better than others, and only those at the very top of the healthy foods list constitute superfoods. In addition, all superfoods must meet one or more of the following requirements:

✔ They must contain copious amounts of essential nutrients, vitamins, and minerals such as: healthy fats, carbohydrates, dietary fiber, natural sugar and protein, vitamins A, B6, C, and K, and minerals like selenium and manganese.

✔ They must be filled with phytochemicals. Phyto is an antecedent word that means plant. Phytochemicals are important because they make antioxidants. Antioxidants are essential in protecting cells from damage by eliminating free radicals in your bloodstream.

✔ They must be a generous source of omega-3 fatty acids. These essential compounds are found mostly in fish, both fresh- and saltwater. Evidence suggests that fatty coldwater fish, such as salmon, herring, sardines, and mackerel, are best. Omega-3 fatty acids can also be found in fortified eggs, flax seeds, and walnuts.

The benefits of omega-3 fatty acids are numerous:

- ✔ They are generally necessary for human health and cannot be manufactured by the human body.
- ✔ They are crucial in proper brain function and normal growth and development.
- ✔ They are important for proper cognitive and behavioral function.
- ✔ They lower the risk of heart disease.
- ✔ They reduce inflammation in human tissues. This is enormously important because inflammation is the major component of chronic diseases.

The superfoods used to create the recipes in *Skinny Ms. Superfoods* include:

• Almonds	• Carrots	• Grapefruit	• Pecans
• Apples	• Cauliflower	• Green Peas	• Pineapple
• Artichokes	• Cherries	• Green Tea	• Pine Nuts
• Asparagus	• Coconut: milk, flakes, oil	• Honey	• Pistachios
• Avocados		• Kale	• Pumpkin Seeds
• Bananas	• Dark Chocolate	• Kiwi	• Quinoa
• Beets	• Dates	• Legumes	• Spinach
• Bell Peppers	• Eggs	• Lemons	• Squash
• Berries: all types	• Fennel	• Mangoes	• Strawberries
• Broccoli	• Fish: especially salmon	• Mushrooms	• Sweet Potatoes
• Brown Rice		• Oats	• Tomatoes
• Brussels Sprouts	• Flax Seeds	• Onion Family	• Walnuts
• Cabbage	• Garlic	• Oranges	• Yogurt

While not all recipes in this book are low in fats or carbohydrates, all of them are high in various nutrients that contribute to good health.

Can I substitute other products in place of some of the natural foods or low-fat foods in the recipes? Yes, while we at Skinny Ms. encourage you to eat natural foods and unrefined sweeteners, we know that some people prefer sugar over honey, molasses, or maple syrup. You may use equal amounts of sugar, brown sugar, or Splenda granules in place of the amount of natural unrefined sweeteners called for in our recipes. You may also substitute whole dairy products in place of low-fat or nonfat dairy products that we use in our recipes. In place of coconut oil or safflower oil, you may prefer to use butter instead, which will work fine as a replacement. This cookbook is all about superfoods. However you prefer to incorporate them into your lifestyle, we encourage you to eat more of them, and reap the benefits!

Skinny Ms. thanks you again for choosing our cookbook and wish you the very best in healthy living now and in the future. Enjoy!

—Tiffany McCauley and Gale Compton

Smoothies

Peanut Butter Banana Smoothie

Peanut Butter Banana Smoothie

YIELD: 2 SERVINGS   SERVING SIZE: 1 CUP

This smoothie will fill you up and keep you satisfied all morning long. It's higher in fats, so you'll need to balance out your daily fat intake accordingly. If sodium is a concern, try using plain, nonfat Greek-style yogurt instead of the cottage cheese.

½ cup low-fat cottage cheese

1 medium-size ripe banana

¼ cup fat-free milk

2 tablespoons peanut butter, no sugar added

Honey to taste (optional)

Add all ingredients to a blender, blend well, and serve.

NUTRITIONAL DATA
Data does not include honey.

Calories: 207	Sodium: 285mg
Total Fat: 9g	Carbohydrates: 21g
Saturated Fat: 2g	Dietary Fiber: 2g
Trans Fat: 0g	Sugars: 12g
Cholesterol: 6mg	Protein: 12g

Almond Bliss Smoothie

YIELD: 2 SERVINGS   SERVING SIZE: 1 CUP

Always leave the skins on almonds to get the full benefit of disease-fighting flavonoids. These antioxidants help to prevent cell damage, fight inflammation, and may reduce the risk of cancer.

14 raw almonds, with skins

1 banana, frozen

1 organic apple, cored, with peeling

½ cup low-fat milk (almond or soy can be used in place of regular milk)

¼ cup plain, nonfat Greek-style yogurt

2 teaspoons honey

¼ teaspoon almond extract

Add all ingredients to a blender, blend well, and serve.

NUTRITIONAL DATA

Calories: 182	Sodium: 45mg
Total Fat: 4g	Carbohydrates: 31g
Saturated Fat: 1g	Dietary Fiber: 5g
Trans Fat: 0g	Sugars: 21g
Cholesterol: 4mg	Protein: 7g

Dark Chocolate Cherry Smoothie with Almonds

YIELD: 3 SERVINGS   SERVING SIZE: 1 CUP

Dark chocolate is a very good source of flavonoids, which may help in the fight against heart disease and cancer. Enjoy this smoothie as an afternoon pick me up or a breakfast drink that provides loads of energy throughout the morning.

½ ounce unsweetened baking chocolate, melted
1½ cups frozen dark cherries
⅓ cup lite coconut milk
½ cup low-fat milk
12 raw almonds, with skins

Melt chocolate according to instructions on package. Add all ingredients to a blender; blend until smooth. Add ice, if desired.

NUTRITIONAL DATA

Calories: 175
Total Fat: 10g
Saturated Fat: 5g
Trans Fat: 0g
Cholesterol: 2mg
Sodium: 40mg
Carbohydrates: 20g
Dietary Fiber: 4g
Sugars: 14g
Protein: 6g

Strawberries and Chocolate Smoothie

YIELD: 3½ SERVINGS   SERVING SIZE: 1 CUP

This classic flavor combination will give you a nice supply of fiber, magnesium, and iron as well as vitamin C. Enjoy for breakfast or a really yummy snack!

2 cups plain, nonfat Greek-style yogurt

2 cups halved and stemmed strawberries

1 tablespoon unsweetened dark cocoa powder (unsweetened regular cocoa powder is fine, too)

3 tablespoons honey, or to taste

½ teaspoon ground cinnamon

Add all ingredients to a blender, blend well, and serve.

NUTRITIONAL DATA

Calories: 208	Sodium: 46mg
Total Fat: 4g	Carbohydrates: 40g
Saturated Fat: 2g	Dietary Fiber: 10g
Trans Fat: 0g	Sugars: 11g
Cholesterol: 0mg	Protein: 18g

Piña Colada Smoothie

Piña Colada Smoothie

YIELD: 3 SERVINGS   SERVING SIZE: 1 CUP

Low in sodium and no cholesterol, this smoothie is a fantastic source of vitamin C. Refreshing and tropical, this smoothie is sure to put a spring in your step.

1 cup lite coconut milk

2 cups pineapple chunks

2 tablespoons honey (if the pineapple isn't very sweet)

Enough ice to make it icy

Add all ingredients to a blender, blend well, and serve.

> **NUTRITIONAL DATA**
>
> | | |
> |---|---|
> | Calories: 115 | Sodium: 37mg |
> | Total Fat: 5g | Carbohydrates: 16g |
> | Saturated Fat: 4g | Dietary Fiber: 0g |
> | Trans Fat: 0g | Sugars: 14g |
> | Cholesterol: 0mg | Protein: 1g |

Summertime Lemonade Smoothie

YIELD: 2½ SERVINGS   SERVING SIZE: 1 CUP

Enjoy a relaxed summer afternoon . . . for breakfast. This smoothie is higher in sugars, so enjoy occasionally as a special treat. With no cholesterol, fat, or saturated fat, this smoothie will fill you up without weighing you down.

2 cups plain, nonfat Greek-style yogurt

2 tablespoons fresh lemon zest

2 tablespoons fresh lemon juice

¼ cup honey

Add all ingredients to a blender, blend well, and serve.

> **NUTRITIONAL DATA**
>
> | | |
> |---|---|
> | Calories: 202 | Sodium: 58mg |
> | Total Fat: 0g | Carbohydrates: 34g |
> | Saturated Fat: 0g | Dietary Fiber: 0g |
> | Trans Fat: 0g | Sugars: 32g |
> | Cholesterol: 0mg | Protein: 18g |

Orange Power Smoothie

YIELD: 3 SERVINGS   SERVING SIZE: 1 CUP

Fall in love with this amazingly thick and creamy smoothie that is filled with the power of orange goodness. If it's weight you want to lose, then eat a brightly colored member of the morning glory family . . . the sweet potato.

1 cup mashed cooked sweet potato
1 cup pineapple chunks, no sugar added
1 cup freshly squeezed orange juice
1 tablespoon honey
6–8 ice cubes

Peel medium sweet potato, cut into 2-inch cubes, place in a steamer, and steam until tender.

Add sweet potato with next 3 ingredients to a blender, and blend until well combined. Add ice, and continue blending until smooth.

NUTRITIONAL DATA
Calories: 137
Total Fat: 0g
Saturated Fat: 0g
Trans Fat: 0g
Cholesterol: 0mg
Sodium: 22mg
Carbohydrates: 33g
Dietary Fiber: 3g
Sugars: 22g
Protein: 2g

Everything-But-The-Kitchen-Sink Smoothie

YIELD: 5 SERVINGS   SERVING SIZE: 1 CUP

When you add this many fruits and veggies to your morning smoothie, you feel energized all morning thanks to the burst of vitamins C, K, and A, as well as manganese, riboflavin, calcium, and potassium you get. You just can't beat fruits and veggies for starting your day off right!

½ cup plain, nonfat Greek-style yogurt

1½ cups fat-free milk

½ cup frozen strawberries

½ cup frozen pineapple chunks

½ cup frozen spinach, or 2 cups raw

1 medium banana

½ cup frozen mango

½ cup frozen blueberries

Add all ingredients to a blender, blend well, and serve.

Note: If using all frozen produce, it may be best to blend this in a food processor instead of a blender, which may not be able to handle all the frozen produce. Also, be sure none of the frozen fruit is sweetened. If using all fresh produce, reduce milk, and add as needed to reach desired consistency.

NUTRITIONAL DATA	
Calories: 95	Sodium: 49mg
Total Fat: 0g	Carbohydrates: 19g
Saturated Fat: 0g	Dietary Fiber: 2g
Trans Fat: 0g	Sugars: 14g
Cholesterol: 1mg	Protein: 6g

Strawberry Mango Smoothie with a Hint of Summer Basil

YIELD: 3 SERVINGS   SERVING SIZE: 1 CUP

The summer basil makes for a refreshing smoothie and has just the right amount of sweetness. Mangoes have antioxidant properties like vitamin C and phytochemicals.

1 cup mango chunks (1 large mango)
1 cup frozen strawberries
2 fresh summer basil leaves
½ cup plain, nonfat Greek-style yogurt
½ cup low-fat milk
1 tablespoon honey

Add all ingredients to a blender, and blend until smooth. Add additional milk for a thinner consistency, if desired.

NUTRITIONAL DATA
Calories: 102
Total Fat: 1g
Saturated Fat: 0g
Trans Fat: 0g
Cholesterol: 3mg
Sodium: 41mg
Carbohydrates: 19g
Dietary Fiber: 3g
Sugars: 15g
Protein: 6g

Apple-Grape Green Tea Smoothie with Gingerroot

YIELD: 3 SERVINGS   SERVING SIZE: 1 CUP

This is a perfect breakfast smoothie filled with superfoods to give you tons of energy that lasts for hours. In addition, enjoy the refreshing taste and an abundance of vitamin C and manganese.

1 cup seedless red or black grapes, frozen

1 organic apple (Honey Crisp or Gala), cored, with peeling

½ cup plain, nonfat Greek-style yogurt

1 teaspoon freshly grated gingerroot

½ cup unsweetened, home-brewed green tea (Sencha is a good choice)

1 tablespoon honey

1 tablespoon wheat germ

6–8 ice cubes

Add all ingredients to a blender, and blend until smooth. Add additional ice for a thicker smoothie.

NUTRITIONAL DATA
Calories: 130
Total Fat: 1g
Saturated Fat: 0g
Trans Fat: 0g
Cholesterol: 2mg
Sodium: 23mg
Carbohydrates: 27g
Dietary Fiber: 3g
Sugars: 21g
Protein: 5g

Blackberry and Pomegranate Green Tea Smoothie

Blackberry and Pomegranate Green Tea Smoothie

YIELD: 3 SERVINGS   SERVING SIZE: 1 CUP

This superfood smoothie is rich with antioxidants and heart-healthy folate. Trying to get more fiber in your diet? Have one of these smoothies, which are high in dietary fiber and vitamin K.

1¼ cups frozen blackberries
1 cup green tea, no sugar added
½ cup 100% pure pomegranate juice, no sugar added
6–8 ice cubes

Add all ingredients to a blender, blend well, and serve.

NUTRITIONAL DATA

Calories: 52	Sodium: 4mg
Total Fat: 0g	Carbohydrates: 13g
Saturated Fat: 0g	Dietary Fiber: 3g
Trans Fat: 0g	Sugars: 9g
Cholesterol: 0mg	Protein: 1g

Blueberry Delight

YIELD: 2 SERVINGS   SERVING SIZE: 1 CUP

This delightful and nutritious smoothie is one you'll enjoy for years to come. Note that the sodium in cottage cheese is naturally high, so if this is an issue for you, feel free to sub with plain, nonfat Greek-style yogurt.

1 cup frozen blueberries
1 cup low-fat cottage cheese
Juice of ½ a lemon
1 tablespoon honey
½ teaspoon ground cinnamon

Add all ingredients to a blender, blend well, and serve.

NUTRITIONAL DATA

Calories: 176	Sodium: 391mg
Total Fat: 3g	Carbohydrates: 24g
Saturated Fat: 2g	Dietary Fiber: 2g
Trans Fat: 0g	Sugars: 19g
Cholesterol: 10mg	Protein: 13g

Fruity Spinach and Green Tea Smoothie

YIELD: 4 SERVINGS   SERVING SIZE: 1 CUP

Enjoy this sweet and creamy smoothie without an ounce of refined sugar. Creamy Greek-style yogurt fights inflammation. Spinach may help prevent age-related macular degeneration and reduce the risk of Alzheimer's disease.

2 organic apples, cored, with peeling

1 frozen banana

1 cup chopped baby spinach, packed

1 teaspoon grated gingerroot

½ cup plain, nonfat Greek-style yogurt

¾ cup freshly brewed green tea, chilled, unsweetened

6–8 cubes of ice

Add all ingredients to a blender, and blend until smooth and creamy.

NUTRITIONAL DATA
Calories: 86
Total Fat: 0g
Saturated Fat: 0g
Trans Fat: 0g
Cholesterol: 1mg
Sodium: 23mg
Carbohydrates: 19g
Dietary Fiber: 3g
Sugars: 12g
Protein: 4g

Fountain of Youth Smoothie

YIELD: 4 SERVINGS   SERVING SIZE: 1 CUP

What better name for a smoothie that tops the superfoods' list? This recipe is one the entire family will enjoy, including the kids. Kale and spinach provide rich immune-boosting qualities, while the banana and honeydew melon take over the taste.

1 avocado, peeled, seeded
⅛ honeydew melon, cut into about 10 (1-inch) cubes
1 banana, frozen
1 kiwi, peeled
1 cup baby spinach
1 cup chopped green kale, stems removed
½ cup low-fat milk

Add all ingredients to a blender, and blend until smooth. Add additional milk for a thinner consistency, if desired.

NUTRITIONAL DATA
Calories: 162
Total Fat: 8g
Saturated Fat: 2g
Trans Fat: 0g
Cholesterol: 1mg
Sodium: 36mg
Carbohydrates: 22g
Dietary Fiber: 6g
Sugars: 11g
Protein: 4g

Morning Cuppa Joe Smoothie

YIELD: 1½ CUPS   SERVING SIZE: 1 CUP

A cup of coffee in the morning is pretty standard for most of us. But why not add a little extra nutrition like folate and manganese, as well as vitamins A and K to that morning cuppa joe?

1 teaspoon instant coffee
½ cup low-fat cottage cheese
1 cup raw spinach
¼ cup nonfat milk
1 teaspoon vanilla extract
Ice cubes
Honey to taste (optional)

Add all ingredients to a blender, blend well, and serve.

NUTRITIONAL DATA
Data does not include honey.

Calories: 94	Sodium: 294mg
Total Fat: 2g	Carbohydrates: 6g
Saturated Fat: 2g	Dietary Fiber: 0g
Trans Fat: 0g	Sugars: 6g
Cholesterol: 8mg	Protein: 10g

Appetizers and Snacks

Balsamic Strawberry Salsa

Balsamic Strawberry Salsa

YIELD: 8 SERVINGS   SERVING SIZE: ½ CUP

Serve this appetizer at your next dinner party and you may have trouble getting people to sit down for dinner! The vitamin C and fiber are wonderful additions to any healthy eating plan, and you'll get a little protein from the yogurt as well!

4 cups chopped strawberries
½ cup plain, nonfat Greek-style yogurt (regular nonfat yogurt will work as well)
2 tablespoons balsamic vinegar
¼ cup honey

Combine ingredients, and mix well. Serve with 2–4 batches Whole-Grain Cinnamon Pita Chips (page 39), depending on how many people you are serving.

NUTRITIONAL DATA	
Calories: 68	Sodium: 6mg
Total Fat: 0g	Carbohydrates: 16g
Saturated Fat: 0g	Dietary Fiber: 2g
Trans Fat: 0g	Sugars: 13g
Cholesterol: 0mg	Protein: 2g

Strawberry Pineapple Salsa

YIELD: 4 SERVINGS   SERVING SIZE: ½ CUP

With zero fat and cholesterol, and almost no sodium, this salsa is a wonderful and flavorful way to meet your healthy carb quota for the day. Packed with vitamin C and fiber, this is sure to become a family favorite.

1 cup chopped pineapple
1 cup chopped strawberries
½ teaspoon ground cinnamon
¼ teaspoon ground ginger

Mix everything together, and serve with Whole-Grain Cinnamon Pita Chips (page 39) for a delicious snack.

NUTRITIONAL DATA	
Calories: 34	Sodium: 1mg
Total Fat: 0g	Carbohydrates: 9g
Saturated Fat: 0g	Dietary Fiber: 2g
Trans Fat: 0g	Sugars: 6g
Cholesterol: 0mg	Protein: 0g

Fresh Cilantro Salsa

Fresh Cilantro Salsa

YIELD: 2½ CUPS   SERVING SIZE: ½ CUP

Fresh salsa is a beautiful thing. Exceptionally low in sodium, saturated fat and cholesterol, it's also a great source for fiber, phosphorus, vitamins A,C,K, and B6! So dig in with some healthy, whole grain crackers for a delicious and nutritious snack.

2 cup finely chopped tomatoes

½ cup finely chopped sweet onion red onion

½ cup chopped, fresh cilantro

8 garlic cloves, chopped

Salt and pepper to taste

Jalapeño pepper (optional and according to taste)

NUTRITIONAL DATA

Calories: 28	Sodium: 7mg
Total Fat: 0g	Carbohydrates: 6g
Saturated Fat: 0g	Dietary fiber: 1g
Trans Fat: 0g	Sugars: 3g
Cholesterol: 0mg	Protein: 1g

Mix all ingredients together and serve.

Almond Butter Yogurt Dip

YIELD: 12 SERVINGS   SERVING SIZE: 2 TABLESPOONS

Yogurt has active live cultures that may help improve the immune system and lower cholesterol. This three-ingredient recipe has zero grams saturated fat and cholesterol.

½ cup plain, nonfat Greek-style yogurt

¼ cup natural almond butter, crunchy recommended

2 teaspoons honey

NUTRITIONAL DATA

Calories: 40	Sodium: 6mg
Total Fat: 3g	Carbohydrates: 2g
Saturated Fat: 0g	Dietary Fiber: 0g
Trans Fat: 0g	Sugars: 1g
Cholesterol: 0mg	Protein: 2g

Combine all the ingredients in a small bowl; refrigerate until ready to eat.

Serve with your favorite fruit or veggie.

Curry Greek-Style Yogurt Dip

YIELD: 1 SERVING   SERVING SIZE: ½ CUP

With no fat or cholesterol, this delicious dip gives you all the nutritious benefits of Greek-style yogurt without adding to your waistline. Serve with whole-grain crackers or veggies for a wonderfully flavorful snack or appetizer.

½ cup plain, nonfat Greek-style yogurt

¼ teaspoon curry powder

¼ teaspoon cinnamon

¼ teaspoon onion powder

¼ teaspoon garlic powder

1 teaspoon honey

Salt to taste

NUTRITIONAL DATA

Calories: 88	Sodium: 36mg
Total Fat: 0g	Carbohydrates: 11g
Saturated Fat: 0g	Dietary Fiber: 0g
Trans Fat: 0g	Sugars: 9g
Cholesterol: 0mg	Protein: 11g

Blend everything together using a whisk, and serve with whole-grain crackers or vegetables.

Mediterranean Tzatziki Yogurt Sauce

YIELD: 16 SERVINGS   SERVING SIZE: 2 TABLESPOONS

Yogurt is one of the most versatile superfoods available. Some of the health benefits of yogurt include being high in protein, calcium, and riboflavin. Yogurt's active bacteria cultures may help to lower cholesterol.

1 medium cucumber, peeled, sliced in half lengthwise

1 tablespoon chopped fresh dill, removed from stem

½ teaspoon black pepper

¼ teaspoon sea or kosher salt

¼ teaspoon paprika

1 tablespoon freshly squeezed lemon juice

1 tablespoon extra virgin olive oil

2 garlic cloves, minced

1 cup plain, nonfat Greek-style yogurt

Additional salt to taste

NUTRITIONAL DATA

Calories: 18
Total Fat: 1g
Saturated Fat: 0g
Trans Fat: 0g
Cholesterol: 1mg
Sodium: 34mg
Carbohydrates: 1g
Dietary Fiber: 1g
Sugars: 1g
Protein: 1g

Remove seeds from the center of each cucumber by scooping out with a spoon. Dice seeded cucumber, and lay pieces on a paper towel to drain; sprinkle with salt.

After 30 minutes, place diced cucumbers and the remaining ingredients in a mixing bowl, and stir. For a smoother sauce, add ingredients to a food processor, and pulse for 3 seconds. Refrigerate at least 2 hours before serving, allowing flavors time to meld. Pour into a serving dish and enjoy! Tastes equally great served with meat.

Creamy Avocado-Yogurt Spread

YIELD: 5 SERVINGS   SERVING SIZE: ¼ CUP

This recipe is high in protein and dietary fiber. Avocados may help lower LDL, or bad choles-
terol. Also, count on a rich and creamy spread that is low in sodium and cholesterol, while
high in copper and vitamin C.

2 avocados, peeled, seeds removed
1 small shallot
1 garlic clove
¼ cup plain, nonfat Greek-style yogurt
Juice of 1 lime
¼ cup chopped fresh cilantro
1 jalapeño chile
¼ teaspoon cumin
¼ teaspoon ground coriander seed
¼ teaspoon black pepper
Salt to taste

NUTRITIONAL DATA
Calories: 59
Total Fat: 4g
Saturated Fat: 1g
Trans Fat: 0g
Cholesterol: 1mg
Sodium: 30mg
Carbohydrates: 4g
Dietary Fiber: 2g
Sugars: 1g
Protein: 2g

Add all ingredients to a food processor. Pulse until ingredients are combined and
spread is a smooth consistency. Refrigerate until ready to eat.

Guacamole Verde

YIELD: 6 SERVINGS   SERVING SIZE: ½ CUP

Avocados are naturally high in fat, but it's healthy fat, which aids in overall health and bodily functions. Enjoy in moderation, but do include healthy fats in your eating plan. This recipe is a great way to do just that. There's no cholesterol, and it's filled with fiber as well as vitamins C and K.

4 medium avocados

1 cup chunky verde sauce, no sugar added

1 teaspoon garlic powder

Juice of ½ lemon

Mash all ingredients together, and serve.

NUTRITIONAL DATA	
Calories: 234	Sodium: 278mg
Total Fat: 20g	Carbohydrates: 14g
Saturated Fat: 3g	Dietary Fiber: 9g
Trans Fat: 0g	Sugars: 3g
Cholesterol: 0mg	Protein: 3g

Note: Yield will vary based on size of avocados.

Roasted Bell Pepper and Sun-Dried Tomato Spread with Sweet Basil

Roasted Bell Pepper and Sun-Dried Tomato Spread with Sweet Basil

YIELD: 14 SERVINGS   SERVING SIZE: 2 TABLESPOONS

This recipe is versatile enough to be a spread, or a rich tomato paste used in place of sauce on pizza crust. Add to pasta dishes, or try in your favorite chili recipe. Regardless of how you choose to use this delicious spread, enjoy the added benefits of it being low in cholesterol and having high amounts of vitamins A, B6, C, and K.

1 red bell pepper, seeded and cored

1 orange bell pepper, seeded and cored

2 teaspoons extra virgin olive oil

1 (8-ounce) jar sun-dried tomatoes packed in olive oil

¼ cup fresh sweet basil, packed

Sea salt to taste

NUTRITIONAL DATA	
Calories: 34	Sodium: 21mg
Total Fat: 2g	Carbohydrates: 3g
Saturated Fat: 0g	Dietary Fiber: 1g
Trans Fat: 0g	Sugars: 1g
Cholesterol: 0mg	Protein: 1g

Preheat oven to 400°.

Cut bell peppers into fourths, and place on a cookie sheet lined with foil; drizzle with extra virgin olive oil. Roast 20 minutes. Allow to cool, and remove skins, if desired.

While bell peppers are roasting, add sun-dried tomatoes and garlic to a medium skillet; sauté until tomatoes soften up, about 4 minutes. Add basil, and toss until wilted; remove from heat, drain oil, and cool 5 minutes.

Add cooled roasted bell peppers and sun-dried tomato mixture to a food processor. Pulse until all ingredients are combined and spread is a smooth consistency.

Tip: This is wonderful spread on whole-grain artisan bread, sprinkled with mozzarella cheese, and toasted in a 425° oven until melted.

Sun-Dried Tomato and Artichoke Spread

YIELD: 18 SERVINGS   SERVING SIZE: 2 TABLESPOONS

I love the versatility of this spread. Try using this in place of mayonnaise on most sandwiches, or add to a vegetable tray at your next office function. Tomatoes contain a pigment called lycopene, which is widely believed to inhibit the growth of cancer cells. When buying sundried tomatoes, always look for the ones bottled in olive oil, which increase the benefits of lycopene.

1 teaspoon olive oil

2 garlic cloves, minced

½ cup sun-dried tomatoes

1 (8-ounce) can artichoke hearts, drained

½ cup freshly grated Parmesan cheese

½ cup plain, nonfat Greek-style yogurt

1 (8-ounce) container fat-free cream cheese, softened

1 tablespoon chopped fresh thyme, stem removed

Salt to taste

> NUTRITIONAL DATA
> Calories: 31
> Total Fat: 1g
> Saturated Fat: 0g
> Trans Fat: 0g
> Cholesterol: 3mg
> Sodium: 17mg
> Carbohydrates: 2g
> Dietary Fiber: 0g
> Sugars: 1g
> Protein: 3g

Add oil to a small skillet; sauté garlic over medium-low heat until tender, about 4 minutes. Add garlic and remaining ingredients to a food processor; pulse until smooth.

Store dip in a glass container with lid; refrigerate at least 2 hours. Serve with vegetables or your favorite whole-grain crackers.

Whole-Grain Cinnamon Pita Chips

YIELD: 12 SERVINGS   SERVING SIZE: 8 CHIPS OR 1 PITA

1 (12-count) package whole-wheat pitas
¼ cup honey
2 teaspoons cinnamon

Cut the stack of pita bread into eighths like you would a pizza. Spread them in a single layer on a lightly greased cookie sheet, keeping them pushed together as much as possible. The less room you have between them the better.

Drizzle the honey over the top, and then sprinkle the cinnamon over that.

Bake at 350° for approximately 15 minutes, or until the pitas are hard, like chips. Note that they will harden a bit further as they cool. If you take them out too soon and find that they did not harden enough, simply return to the oven until they are baked to your liking.

Note: Data will vary based on whole-wheat pitas used. Check different brands to lower sodium.

NUTRITIONAL DATA
Calories: 193
Total Fat: 2g
Saturated Fat: 0g
Trans Fat: 0g
Cholesterol: 0mg
Sodium: 341mg
Carbohydrates: 41g
Dietary Fiber: 5g
Sugars: 6g
Protein: 6g

Stuffed Mushrooms

YIELD: 7 SERVINGS   SERVING SIZE: 3 MUSHROOMS

These delicious mushrooms are sure to please. Packed with vitamins A, C, B6, calcium, and iron as well as potassium and zinc, you'll love every healthy bite.

1¼ pounds brown mushrooms
½ large red bell pepper, finely chopped
4 large garlic cloves, minced
½ cup grated Parmesan cheese
1 teaspoon dried parsley

Remove stems from mushrooms, and chop to use in filling, if desired. Combine next 4 ingredients. Add chopped stems, if desired. Stuff mushrooms with filling, and place on a parchment-lined cookie sheet. Bake at 350° for 30–40 minutes, or until mushrooms are soft and cooked.

NUTRITIONAL DATA

Calories: 59	Sodium: 115mg
Total Fat: 2g	Carbohydrates: 5g
Saturated Fat: 1g	Dietary Fiber: 1g
Trans Fat: 0g	Sugars: 2g
Cholesterol: 6mg	Protein: 5g

Note: Nutritional data for mushrooms will vary depending on the size and number of mushrooms in 1¼ pounds. We had 21 mushrooms, so the data here reflects that. Allow for some wiggle room in the numbers. Remember, these are appetizers, not a meal.

Candied Pecans

YIELD: 18 SERVINGS   SERVING SIZE: 6 PECANS

These sweet pecans are a perfect snack food or salad topper. Pecans are an excellent source of manganese, which helps to protect against viruses and other infections by helping to strengthen our cell walls. Grab a handful of pecans on a daily basis, and lower your risk of heart disease.

1 egg white, slightly beaten
1 teaspoon water
4 cups pecans
⅓ cup honey

Preheat oven to 325°.

Place parchment paper on a cookie sheet. In a large mixing bowl, combine egg white and water; beat slightly with a fork. Add pecans; coat thoroughly with egg white. Pour honey over pecans, and toss to combine.

NUTRITIONAL DATA
Calories: 186
Total Fat: 15g
Saturated Fat: 1.5g
Trans Fat: 0g
Cholesterol: 0mg
Sodium: 2mg
Carbohydrates: 6g
Dietary Fiber: 2g
Sugars: 3g
Protein: 2g

Spread pecans onto parchment-lined cookie sheet, making sure they are not stacked. Bake 15 minutes, or until lightly roasted. Allow pecans to cool completely before storing in an airtight container.

Lemon Flax Seed Energy Balls

Lemon Flax Seed Energy Balls

YIELD: 68 SERVINGS   SERVING SIZE: 1 ENERGY BALL

Need to power through your workout? These should do the trick! Filled with good-for-you ingredients, these energy balls will get you through that workout without the nervous "tick" that caffeine can provide. These little goodies have no cholesterol, are very low in sodium, and are a wonderful source of manganese and copper.

1 cup cashews (we used raw cashews, but roasted are fine)

14 large medjool dates, chopped

2 tablespoons flax seeds

Juice and zest of 1 small lemon

⅓ cup shredded coconut

Blend cashews, dates, flax seeds, lemon juice, and zest together in a food processor until the mix turns into a soft ball. If the mixture is overly sticky, place in a bowl and store in the freezer for an hour.

Using your hands, form equal-sized balls (about the size of half a walnut). Roll in coconut, and place in a storage container. Store in the refrigerator.

Note: Because these are a snack, we felt it was better to give the data for 1 energy ball. You will eat more than that, so simply multiply the data by the number you eat.

NUTRITIONAL DATA
Calories: 59
Total Fat: 2g
Saturated Fat: 1g
Trans Fat: 0g
Cholesterol: 6mg
Sodium: 115mg
Carbohydrates: 5g
Dietary Fiber: 1g
Sugars: 2g
Protein: 5g

Granola Crunch

YIELD: 12 SERVINGS   SERVING SIZE: ½ CUP

Pure superfood goodness best describes this yummy granola, which makes a great bowl of breakfast cereal, yogurt topping, pre-workout snack, and a school or work midday pick me up. Making your own granola is a great way to control the amount of sugar and sodium. When a touch of sweetness is needed, we use only natural sweeteners, never refined, and that you can count on.

4 cups old-fashioned oats
¼ cup raw pumpkin seeds
¾ cup raw almonds, with skins, sliced in half
¾ cup raw walnuts, coarsely chopped
¼ cup wheat germ
1 teaspoon cinnamon
⅓ cup extra virgin coconut oil
¼ cup honey
¼ cup pure maple syrup

NUTRITIONAL DATA
Calories: 477
Total Fat: 21g
Saturated Fat: 7g
Trans Fat: 0g
Cholesterol: 0mg
Sodium: 2mg
Carbohydrates: 60g
Dietary Fiber: 9g
Sugars: 12g
Protein: 15g

Preheat oven to 350°.

In a large mixing bowl, combine the first 6 ingredients. Add oil, honey, and maple syrup to a small bowl, and whisk to combine. Pour wet ingredients over oat mixture, and stir to combine, until all dry ingredients are moist.

Line 2 large rimmed cookie sheets with parchment paper. Evenly distribute oat mixture, place in oven, and stir after 15 minutes; reverse position of cookie sheets. Continue baking another 10–15 minutes or until cereal is golden in color. Cool completely. Store in an airtight container up to 1 week.

For best results, do not store dried fruit with cereal, as it tends to add moisture.

Tip: Some great additions to Granola Crunch: dried Bing cherries, raisins, coconut, blueberries, or just about any dried or fresh berry.

Breakfast

Apple Zucchini Waffles

Apple Zucchini Waffles

YIELD: 6 SERVINGS   SERVING SIZE: 1 WAFFLE

These large, Belgian-sized waffles are a sure way to get your morning off to a sweet start. Top with honey or maple syrup and you've got a deliciously healthy way to get a nice helping of fiber, protein, and calcium, as well as riboflavin and selenium.

2 cups white whole-wheat flour

2½ cups fat-free milk (nondairy milk works, too)

2 teaspoons baking powder

2 egg whites

¾ cup grated apple

1 cup grated zucchini

2 teaspoons pure vanilla extract

Blend everything together in a large mixing bowl, and cook in a waffle maker as directed by appliance instructions. Note that this batter is thicker than most, and you may have to help it spread a bit before closing the waffle maker.

Tip: We used a Belgian waffle maker for these, so they are large waffles. But any waffle maker will work.

NUTRITIONAL DATA
Calories: 192
Total Fat: 1g
Saturated Fat: 0g
Trans Fat: 0g
Cholesterol: 2mg
Sodium: 224mg
Carbohydrates: 38g
Dietary Fiber: 5g
Sugars: 8g
Protein: 10g

Apple-Pecan Breakfast Crumb Cake

YIELD: 8 SERVINGS   SERVING SIZE: ⅛ OF THE RECIPE

Apples contain phytochemicals that are thought to help prevent the replication of cancer cells. Apples also assist in decreasing cholesterol levels. And, with this breakfast cake chock-full of apples, you can enjoy its health benefits with every bite.

1¼ cups white whole-wheat flour

1 teaspoon baking powder

½ teaspoon baking soda

1 teaspoon cinnamon

½ teaspoon sea salt

½ cup canola oil

½ cup honey

1 large egg, slightly beaten

1 teaspoon vanilla

2 cups organic ½-inch apple pieces (Fuji or Gala are good choices), peeled and cored

½ cup diced pecans

STREUSEL:

2 tablespoons white whole-wheat flour

¼ cup old-fashioned oats

¼ cup finely diced pecans

1 teaspoon cinnamon

1 tablespoon honey

NUTRITIONAL DATA	
Calories: 507	Sodium: 369mg
Total Fat: 0g	Carbohydrates: 50g
Saturated Fat: 3g	Dietary Fiber: 8g
Trans Fat: 0g	Sugars: 20g
Cholesterol: 26mg	Protein: 9g

Preheat oven to 325°.

In a small bowl, combine Streusel ingredients; set aside.

Combine the first 5 ingredients in a small mixing bowl. Next, in a large mixing bowl, add canola oil, honey, egg, and vanilla; beat on medium speed until ingredients are well combined, about 2 minutes. Add apples and pecans to dry ingredients, and stir until combined. Add dry ingredients to wet ingredients, and stir to combine.

Lightly spray an 8-inch round cake pan (or 8x8-inch square cake pan) with nonstick cooking spray, pour batter into pan, and evenly sprinkle Streusel over cake batter. Loosely cover with foil after 30 minutes of baking to prevent Streusel from browning too quickly. Bake 45–50 minutes, or until edges begin to brown and pull away from side of pan.

Allow to cool before serving.

Apple-Cinnamon Pancakes with Dates

YIELD: 7 SERVINGS   SERVING SIZE: 2 PANCAKES

No need for syrup with this recipe. Dates are one of nature's sweetest candies, and its health benefits make this breakfast a superfoods treat.

**1 cup white whole-wheat flour
(or may use whole-wheat flour)**

1 cup oat flour

2¼ teaspoons baking powder

½ teaspoon baking soda

¼ teaspoon salt

1 teaspoon cinnamon

12 almonds, with skins

2 eggs, slightly beaten

¼ cup canola oil

**1 cup finely diced, cored, and
peeled apples**

6 dates, finely diced

1 tablespoon honey

1½ cups buttermilk

NUTRITIONAL DATA

Calories: 396	Sodium: 358mg
Total Fat: 14g	Carbohydrates: 56g
Saturated Fat: 2g	Dietary Fiber: 8g
Trans Fat: 0g	Sugars: 14g
Cholesterol: 63mg	Protein: 12g

In a large mixing bowl, whisk together dry ingredients. In another mixing bowl, combine remaining ingredients. Pour wet mixture into dry, and stir until combined and most lumps disappear.

Heat a griddle to 350° or until a drop of water sizzles when dropped on griddle. Spray griddle or skillet with nonstick cooking spray, and pour in ⅓ cup pancake batter.

Turn pancakes over when they begin to dry around the edges and are golden on the bottom. If desired, top pancakes with additional diced apples, almonds, and a sprinkle of cinnamon. If desired, drizzle with 100% pure maple syrup.

Tip: To make oat flour, add old-fashioned oats to a blender (1 cup oats makes 1 cup flour), and blend until a flour-like consistency is achieved.

Flax Seed Pancakes

YIELD: 6 SERVINGS   **SERVING SIZE: 3 (3-INCH) PANCAKES**

Pancakes can be healthy! With the right mix of ingredients, you get a nice chunk of nutrients in the most important meal of the day. One serving of these pancakes is a great way to start your day with fiber, selenium, manganese, thiamin, phosphorus, and magnesium—and they're low in saturated fat and cholesterol, too.

2 cups white whole-wheat pastry flour

2 egg whites

3 cups milk (we used almond milk, but any milk will work)

¼ cup flax seeds

2 teaspoons vanilla extract

1 teaspoon baking powder (aluminum free)

Whisk all ingredients together, and cook as you would normally, using a nonstick pan.

NUTRITIONAL DATA
Calories: 200
Total Fat: 5g
Saturated Fat: 0g
Trans Fat: 0g
Cholesterol: 0mg
Sodium: 192mg
Carbohydrates: 33g
Dietary Fiber: 7g
Sugars: 1g
Protein: 8g

Whole-Grain Banana Blueberry Pancakes with Walnuts

YIELD: 6 SERVINGS   SERVING SIZE: 2 PANCAKES

These are perfect for a weekend family breakfast. Your family will love these delicious pancakes, and you can feel good about serving up this superfood breakfast. This recipe is a great energy booster, and contains additional fiber and potassium.

1 cup oat flour

1 cup white whole-wheat flour (or may use whole-wheat flour)

2¼ teaspoons baking powder

½ teaspoon baking soda

¼ teaspoon salt

½ cup diced walnuts

2 eggs, slightly beaten

¼ cup canola oil

1 banana, mashed

2 tablespoons honey

1 cup buttermilk

½ cup low-fat milk

½ cup fresh blueberries

NUTRITIONAL DATA	
Calories: 274	Sodium: 38mg
Total Fat: 12g	Carbohydrates: 34g
Saturated Fat: 2g	Dietary Fiber: 4g
Trans Fat: 0g	Sugars: 8g
Cholesterol: 0mg	Protein: 8g

In a large mixing bowl, whisk dry ingredients together. In another mixing bowl, combine remaining ingredients, except blueberries. Pour wet mixture into dry, and stir until combined and most lumps disappear; fold in blueberries.

Heat griddle to 350°, or until a drop of water sizzles when dropped on griddle. Spray griddle with nonstick cooking spray, and pour on ⅓ cup pancake mix.

Turn pancakes over when they begin to dry around the edges and are golden on the bottom. If desired, top pancakes with additional blueberries and bananas, and drizzle with 100% pure maple syrup.

Tip: To make oat flour, add old-fashioned oats to a blender (1 cup oats makes 1 cup flour), and blend until a flour-like consistency is achieved.

Whole-Grain Carrot-Zucchini Muffins

Whole-Grain Carrot-Zucchini Muffins

YIELD: 16 SERVINGS   SERVING SIZE: 1 MUFFIN

This breakfast muffin has only one gram of saturated fat and is very low in cholesterol. The veggies in this muffin, carrots and zucchini, may help in the fight against certain types of cancer.

STREUSEL:

½ cup Granola Crunch (page 44)
1 tablespoon honey

Preheat oven to 350°.

Combine Streusel ingredients in a small bowl, and set aside.

1½ cups white whole-wheat flour
2 tablespoons wheat germ
1 teaspoon baking powder
½ teaspoon baking soda
¼ teaspoon sea salt
1 teaspoon cinnamon
1 cup Granola Crunch (page 44)
  (or may use granola of choice)
⅓ cup canola oil
⅓ cup honey
1 large egg, slightly whipped
1 teaspoon vanilla
½ cup finely shredded zucchini, with
  peeling
½ cup finely shredded carrot, peeled
1 cup low-fat buttermilk

NUTRITIONAL DATA

Calories: 221	Sodium: 266mg
Total Fat: 8g	Carbohydrates: 30g
Saturated Fat: 1g	Dietary Fiber: 3g
Trans Fat: 0g	Sugars: 13g
Cholesterol: 14mg	Protein: 6g

In a large mixing bowl, whisk together dry ingredients; set aside. Add remaining ingredients to a medium mixing bowl, and stir until combined. Pour wet ingredients into dry, and stir just until moist.

Line muffin tin with paper cup holders, or mist with nonstick cooking spray. Fill tins to ⅔ full; add approximately 1 teaspoon Streusel to the top of each muffin. Bake 17 minutes or until a toothpick inserted in the middle comes out clean.

Sweet Potato Biscuits

YIELD: 12 BISCUITS   SERVING SIZE: 1 BISCUIT

Here's a twist on an old standard. These buttermilk biscuits are baked with an added touch of sweetness and the super-healthy addition of sweet potato. Sweet potatoes are a great source of vitamin A and are low in cholesterol. As an excellent complex carbohydrate, sweet potatoes are good for those who need to control their weight . . . so eat up!

4 cups white whole-wheat flour

1½ tablespoons baking powder

1 teaspoon baking soda

½ teaspoon salt

1 teaspoon cinnamon

½ cup coconut oil, solid

1½ cups low-fat buttermilk

1 cup cooked and mashed sweet potato

½ teaspoon vanilla extract

¼ cup honey

TOPPING:

¼ cup honey

½ teaspoon cinnamon

½ cup minced pecans

Preheat oven to 375°.

In a large mixing bowl, whisk together the first 5 ingredients. Using a fork, cut in coconut oil until it resembles coarse crumbs. Make a well in the center of the flour mixture, and add buttermilk; stir just until wet and dry ingredients are moist. It's important not to overmix the dough. In a small bowl, combine mashed sweet potato, vanilla, and honey. Add sweet potato mixture to

NUTRITIONAL DATA	
Calories: 314	Sodium: 249mg
Total Fat: 12g	Carbohydrates: 43g
Saturated Fat: 1g	Dietary Fiber: 6g
Trans Fat: 0g	Sugars: 12g
Cholesterol: 1mg	Protein: 8g

dough, and stir or knead lightly with hands. Again, do not overmix the dough. The sweet potato dough will be a little on the sticky side.

Turn dough onto a lightly floured surface. Flour hands, and gently shape the dough to about a 1-inch thickness (dough will be sticky). Using a 2-inch biscuit cutter, cut biscuits straight down and do not twist. Continue, dipping biscuit cutter in flour before each biscuit cut. Place biscuits onto cookie sheet, touching slightly.

In a small bowl, mix together Topping ingredients. Spread equally on biscuits. Bake 20–25 minutes.

Tip: Lining your cookie sheet with parchment paper will help prevent biscuits from sticking.

Breakfast Burrito

YIELD: 2 SERVINGS   SERVING SIZE: 1 BURRITO

Never underestimate the power of a nutritious breakfast burrito to power you through a busy morning! You'll get a nice portion of protein, vitamins C, B6, and A, and plenty of riboflavin. What a great way to start your morning!

3 large garlic cloves, chopped

2 teaspoons olive oil

2 large whole eggs

2 large egg whites (or 6 egg whites and no whole eggs)

1 cup grated zucchini

1 teaspoon cumin

1 cup chopped tomatoes

2 whole-wheat tortillas

Sauté garlic in olive oil for about 30 seconds over low heat, then add eggs and egg whites along with the zucchini and cumin. Cook eggs until done, stirring constantly. Scoop onto tortilla, top with tomatoes, and wrap your burrito.

> NUTRITIONAL DATA
> Data does not include tortilla.
>
> Calories: 164
> Total Fat: 10g
> Saturated Fat: 2g
> Trans Fat: 0g
> Cholesterol: 211mg
> Sodium: 138mg
> Carbohydrates: 8g
> Dietary Fiber: 2g
> Sugars: 4g
> Protein: 12g

Note: Due to the variance in nutritional data for tortillas, this data is not included. The nutritional data is for the filling only.

Over-Easy Egg with Mushrooms and Roma Tomatoes on Toast

YIELD: 1 SERVING   SERVING SIZE: 1 SANDWICH

Send your family off with a superfoods, nutrient-packed, quick-to-prepare, breakfast. Not only is this breakfast a good source of vitamins A and K, it's also an excellent source of selenium, which may help lower the risk of cancer and heart disease.

2 teaspoons canola oil, divided

½ cup sliced white mushrooms

1 slice whole-grain bread or roll

1 large egg (free-range is best)

Sea salt and freshly ground pepper to taste

1 small Roma tomato, sliced thinly

1 tablespoon grated Parmesan

NUTRITIONAL DATA	
Calories: 290	Sodium: 560mg
Total Fat: 12g	Carbohydrates: 30g
Saturated Fat: 3g	Dietary Fiber: 4g
Trans Fat: 0g	Sugars: 5g
Cholesterol: 216mg	Protein: 17g

Preheat oven to 375°.

Add 1 teaspoon canola oil to a small nonstick skillet; heat to medium-low, and sauté mushrooms until soft, about 6 minutes. Remove from skillet, and set aside.

Place bread on a cookie sheet; toast on one side until golden.

In the same skillet used before, heat to low and add remaining 1 teaspoon canola oil. Add whole egg, seasoned with salt and pepper, to skillet. Turn the skillet from side to side until the white begins to set; then shake to make sure the egg isn't sticking. When the white is set, flip over using a spatula, being careful not to break the yolk. Cook egg until set on the other side.

Add to untoasted side of bread: over-easy egg, mushrooms, and tomato, and top off with Parmesan cheese.

Artichoke and Spinach Frittata

YIELD: 6 SERVINGS   SERVING SIZE: 1 SLICE

Here's one breakfast that's packed with superfoods. Eggs support eye health and brain function and may help protect against macular degeneration and cataracts. Artichokes may help in lowering cholesterol levels and aid in liver function. Spinach may help to reduce inflammation, which is often linked to heart disease and type 2 diabetes. Overall, this breakfast provides a good dose of protein, vitamins A and K, riboflavin, and selenium.

1 garlic clove, minced

¼ cup diced sweet onion

2 teaspoons extra virgin olive oil

1 cup baby spinach

2 eggs (free-range is best)

4 egg whites (free-range is best)

⅓ cup low-fat milk

2 medium (canned) artichoke hearts, diced

½ teaspoon black pepper

¼ cup grated Parmesan cheese

Salt to taste

Preheat oven to broil.

In a large oven-safe skillet, sauté garlic and onion in oil over medium-low heat until tender, about 4 minutes. Add spinach, and continue sautéing until wilted, 1–2 minutes.

NUTRITIONAL DATA	
Calories: 78	Sodium: 182mg
Total Fat: 5g	Carbohydrates: 3g
Saturated Fat: 2g	Dietary Fiber: 0g
Trans Fat: 0g	Sugars: 1g
Cholesterol: 74mg	Protein: 6g

In a medium mixing bowl, whisk together eggs, egg whites, and milk. Add spinach mixture and remaining ingredients; whisk to combine. Pour egg mixture into skillet, and cook on medium heat until eggs pull away from sides and are slightly set, about 5 minutes.

Place skillet under broiler until eggs are set and puffy, but not hard. Remove from oven, and sprinkle with additional Parmesan, if desired. Cut into 6 wedges, and serve immediately.

Crustless Asparagus Quiche

Crustless Asparagus Quiche

YIELD: 8 SERVINGS   SERVING SIZE: 1 SLICE

If you are watching carbs and calories, you really can't do much better for breakfast than this quiche. You'll be getting tons of nutrients as well! This delicious quiche is high in vitamins C, A, and K, iron, and folate, and is a great source of protein. Not too bad for 53 calories per serving!

2 cups sliced asparagus

6 egg whites

2 whole eggs

½ teaspoon garlic powder

½ teaspoon onion powder

¼ cup grated Parmesan cheese

½ cup chopped tomatoes

NUTRITIONAL DATA	
Calories: 53	Sodium: 108mg
Total Fat: 2g	Carbohydrates: 2g
Saturated Fat: 1g	Dietary Fiber: 1g
Trans Fat: 0g	Sugars: 1g
Cholesterol: 56mg	Protein: 6g

Combine ingredients, and pour into greased quiche pan or pie plate.

Bake at 350° for 45–55 minutes, or until the center has no liquid when you cut into it. Note that this will puff up a lot during baking, but will sink down again as it cools.

To serve, cut into 8 wedges.

Variation: You may use 1½ cups egg substitute in place of the eggs and egg whites.

Oven Omelet with Mushrooms and Sun-Dried Tomatoes

YIELD: 4 SERVINGS   SERVING SIZE: ¼ OMELET

In addition to the high protein content of the omelet, it's also a good source of vitamins C and K, riboflavin, and selenium. Vitamin K may help in slowing Alzheimer's disease.

2 teaspoons olive oil

½ cup diced Shiitake mushrooms

2 green onions, diced

¼ cup diced sun-dried tomatoes, packed in olive oil

2 large eggs (free-range is best)

2 large egg whites (free-range is best)

1 tablespoon milk

¼ cup low-fat feta cheese

1 tablespoon grated Parmesan cheese

Salt and pepper to taste

Preheat oven to 350°.

In a medium nonstick skillet, add olive oil. On medium-low heat, sauté mushrooms, green onions, and sun-dried tomatoes until tender, about 4 minutes.

NUTRITIONAL DATA	
Calories: 110	Sodium: 306mg
Total Fat: 6g	Carbohydrates: 6g
Saturated Fat: 1g	Dietary Fiber: 1g
Trans Fat: 0g	Sugars: 1g
Cholesterol: 112mg	Protein: 8

In a medium mixing bowl, whisk together eggs, egg whites, and milk. Add sautéed mushrooms, onions, and tomatoes to eggs; whisk to combine.

Pour egg mixture in the same nonstick skillet, place in oven, and cook until eggs are set but still soft, 12–15 minutes. Add cheeses, and season to taste. The size of skillet used will determine the thickness of the omelet, and may cause cooking time to vary by 1–2 minutes.

Super Fruit Bonanza Oatmeal

YIELD: 6 SERVINGS   SERVING SIZE: 1 CUP

If you enjoy fruit in your morning oatmeal, why not make sure you're getting some of the most nutritious fruit in the process? This dish has no saturated fat or cholesterol and is a great source of fiber and vitamin C, and gives you approximately 51% of your daily manganese requirement. Tough to get that in a boxed cereal!

1½ cups old-fashioned rolled oats (not quick-cooking)

2 tablespoons flax seeds

1 medium ripe banana, mashed

1 medium sweet apple, grated

1 medium mango, peeled, seeded, and chopped

1 cup fresh or frozen blueberries

1 teaspoon cinnamon

2 teaspoons pure vanilla extract

Combine all ingredients in a large baking dish, stir well to combine, and bake at 350° for 1 hour.

Note: Top with fresh sliced strawberries just before serving for an added bonanza.

NUTRITIONAL DATA

Calories: 164
Total Fat: 3g
Saturated Fat: 0g
Trans Fat: 0g
Cholesterol: 0mg
Sodium: 4mg
Carbohydrates: 33g
Dietary Fiber: 5g
Sugars: 14g
Protein: 4g

Flax and Apple Raisin Oatmeal

Flax and Apple Raisin Oatmeal

YIELD: 6 SERVINGS   SERVING SIZE: 1 CUP

Flax seeds and apples just seem to go together. They are warm and comforting first thing in the morning, and with the added health benefits of oats, you can't go wrong. Oats are low in sodium, saturated fat, and cholesterol. They are an excellent way to get manganese, phosphorus, and vitamin A as well.

1 small apple, grated

2 cups old-fashioned rolled oats (not quick-cooking)

4 cups fat-free milk (nondairy works well, too)

½ teaspoon ground cinnamon

¼ cup flax seeds or flax meal

1 cup golden raisins

NUTRITIONAL DATA	
Calories: 292	Sodium: 76mg
Total Fat: 5g	Carbohydrates: 54g
Saturated Fat: 1g	Dietary Fiber: 6g
Trans Fat: 0g	Sugars: 28g
Cholesterol: 3mg	Protein: 11g

Combine all ingredients in a lightly greased 2-quart baking dish. Bake at 350° for 1 hour.

California Hippie Oatmeal

YIELD: 4 SERVINGS   SERVING SIZE: 1 CUP

Enjoy the health benefits of oats with the natural, brown sugar sweetness of dates. The flax seeds will give you lots of omega-3's, and the cinnamon adds a wonderful, comforting flavor. This breakfast has no cholesterol and is a great way to get fiber and manganese.

1½ cups old-fashioned rolled oats (not quick-cooking)

8 medjool dates, seeded and chopped

2 teaspoons flax seeds

1 teaspoon ground cinnamon

NUTRITIONAL DATA	
Calories: 389	Sodium: 3mg
Total Fat: 6g	Carbohydrates: 77g
Saturated Fat: 1g	Dietary Fiber: 11g
Trans Fat: 0g	Sugars: 32g
Cholesterol: 0mg	Protein: 12g

Combine all ingredients in a lightly greased 2-quart baking dish. Bake at 350° for 1 hour.

Strawberry Banana Oatmeal

YIELD: 6 SERVINGS   SERVING SIZE: 1 CUP

When my family tried this combination of ingredients in their morning oatmeal, they discovered a new favorite breakfast food that's not only healthy but has an unbeatable taste. The strawberries in this recipe contain beta carotene, which is an immune booster and may help protect against heart disease.

1 cup steel-cut oats

2 cups water

2 cups 1% milk

2 bananas, sliced

1 tablespoon honey

1 teaspoon cinnamon

10 fresh strawberries

¼ cup minced almonds

NUTRITIONAL DATA

Calories: 208	Sodium: 42mg
Total Fat: 5g	Carbohydrates: 36g
Saturated Fat: 1g	Dietary Fiber: 5g
Trans Fat: 0g	Sugars: 13g
Cholesterol: 3mg	Protein: 8g

In a medium saucepan, combine the first 6 ingredients. Bring mixture to a boil, then reduce heat to a simmer; continue cooking uncovered for 20–25 minutes, or until desired consistency. Add sliced strawberries and almonds, and enjoy!

Weekend Oatmeal with Wheat Germ, Bananas, and Raisins

YIELD: 3 SERVINGS   SERVING SIZE: 1 CUP

Oats and wheat germ are both excellent sources for lowering what's considered bad cholesterol, or LDL. Moreover, this oatmeal recipe is filled with potassium, which helps cells to function normally and also aids in controlling blood pressure.

1 cup water
1 cup low-fat milk
⅓ cup plus 2 tablespoons steel-cut oats
2 tablespoons wheat germ
1 banana, thinly sliced
½ teaspoon cinnamon
1 tablespoon honey
¼ cup raisins

Add the first 7 ingredients to a heavy saucepan, bring to a boil, and reduce heat to a simmer. Continue cooking 20–25 minutes or until desired consistency. Stir in raisins, and serve.

NUTRITIONAL DATA
Calories: 293
Total Fat: 4g
Saturated Fat: 1g
Trans Fat: 0g
Cholesterol: 3mg
Sodium: 44mg
Carbohydrates: 58g
Dietary Fiber: 6g
Sugars: 23g
Protein: 10g

Cherry and Dark Chocolate Oatmeal Bake

YIELD: 8 SERVINGS   SERVING SIZE: ¾ CUP

This low-sodium, no-cholesterol breakfast is sure to please finicky eaters. A single serving will provide about 48% of your daily manganese intake. Top with a little honey or add some extra chocolate chips when baking if you have a serious sweet tooth.

1½ cups rolled oats

½ cup dark chocolate chips (try for at least 70% dark chocolate)

3 cups unsweetened almond milk (any milk will work)

10 ounces frozen cherries

2 teaspoons vanilla extract

1 teaspoon cinnamon

2 tablespoons flax seeds, whole or ground

Mix all together in a lightly greased 9x13-inch baking dish, and bake at 350° for approximately 45 minutes. Cut into 8 equal portions, and serve.

NUTRITIONAL DATA

Calories: 188
Total Fat: 9g
Saturated Fat: 4g
Trans Fat: 0g
Cholesterol: 0mg
Sodium: 72mg
Carbohydrates: 23g
Dietary Fiber: 4g
Sugars: 7g
Protein: 4g

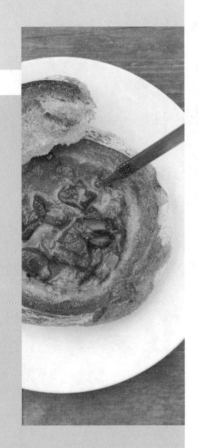

Soups, Stews, and Chilis

15-Bean Soup

15-Bean Soup

YIELD: 10 SERVINGS   SERVING SIZE: 1 CUP

1 (20-ounce) bag 15-bean soup mix, seasoning packet discarded

4 cups low-sodium vegetable broth, no sugar added

8 cups water

2 no-salt vegetable bouillon cubes (we used the Rapunzel brand)

1 cup sliced carrots

1 cup sliced celery

1 tablespoon cumin

2 teaspoons onion powder

2 teaspoons garlic powder

1 teaspoon ground coriander

1 teaspoon paprika

1 tablespoon apple cider vinegar

Salt to taste

NUTRITIONAL DATA
Calories: 225
Total Fat: 2g
Saturated Fat: 1g
Trans Fat: 0g
Cholesterol: 2mg
Sodium: 120mg
Carbohydrates: 41g
Dietary Fiber: 8g
Sugars: 3g
Protein: 13g

Place all ingredients in a large pot, and bring to a boil. Reduce heat to a simmer, and cook for approximately 1½–2 hours or until the beans are fully cooked. Add salt to taste.

Brothy Southwestern 3-Bean Soup

YIELD: 13 SERVINGS   SERVING SIZE: 1 CUP

4 cups low-sodium chicken broth, no sugar added

2 teaspoons garlic powder

2 teaspoons onion powder

2 teaspoons ground cumin

1 teaspoon chili powder

1 cup salsa, no sugar added

1 (15-ounce) can pinto beans, no sugar added, drained and rinsed

1 (15-ounce) can low-sodium black beans, no sugar added, drained and rinsed

1 (15-ounce) can kidney beans, low sodium, no sugar added, drained and rinsed

1 pound frozen corn

1 (28-ounce) can diced tomatoes in juice, no salt added

Salt to taste

In a large soup pot, combine all ingredients, and bring to a gentle simmer. Cook until the corn is cooked through and the beans are warm.

Note: To lower sodium, use low or no-sodium beans, or cook the beans yourself at home with no added salt.

NUTRITIONAL DATA
Calories: 115
Total Fat: 1g
Saturated Fat: 0g
Trans Fat: 0g
Cholesterol: 2mg
Sodium: 336mg
Total Carbohydrate: 23g
Dietary Fiber: 5g
Sugars: 3g
Protein: 6g

Vegetable Lentil Soup

YIELD: 11 SERVINGS   SERVING SIZE: 1 CUP

2½ cups dry, brown lentils, rinsed

9 cups low-sodium vegetable broth, no sugar added

4 cubes vegetable bouillon, no sodium or sugar added (we used Rapunzel brand)

2 cups chopped bell peppers (color of your choice)

¼ pound mushrooms, sliced

1 cup sliced carrots

2 cups cauliflower florets

3 large garlic cloves, chopped

1 teaspoon paprika

Combine all ingredients in a large soup pot. Cook at a simmer, covered, for 50–60 minutes, or until lentils are soft and cooked.

NUTRITIONAL DATA
Sodium content will vary widely based on broth used.
Calories: 200
Total Fat: 2g
Saturated Fat: 1g
Trans Fat: 0g
Cholesterol: 0mg
Sodium: 383mg
Carbohydrates: 33g
Dietary Fiber: 15g
Sugars: 4g
Protein: 13g

Good-For-You Kale Soup

YIELD: 7 SERVINGS   SERVING SIZE: 1 CUP

This quick and easy soup deliciously warms your soul with a plentiful source of vitamins A, C, and K. Indulge in and enjoy this wonderful bowl of good-for-you nutrients that taste simply amazing.

6 cups low-sodium chicken broth, no sugar added

5 cups chopped kale, tightly packed when measuring

1 tablespoon balsamic vinegar

2 no-sodium, vegetable bouillon cubes (we used Rapunzel brand)

1 teaspoon onion powder

1 teaspoon garlic powder

Dried cranberries for garnish

Bring everything except the cranberries to a medium boil in a large soup pot, and cook until the kale has wilted. Allow to cool, and serve topped with dried cranberries, if desired.

NUTRITIONAL DATA
Data does not include cranberries.

Calories: 60
Total Fat: 2g
Saturated Fat: 1g
Trans Fat: 0g
Cholesterol: 4mg
Sodium: 194mg
Carbohydrates: 9g
Dietary Fiber: 1g
Sugars: 1g
Protein: 3g

Cremini Mushroom Soup

YIELD: 6 SERVINGS   SERVING SIZE: 1 CUP

This delicious and comforting soup will keep you coming back for more. And at just 71 calories per cup, having seconds is not a problem. Plus, you'll be getting vitamin B6, vitamin K, and potassium. So dig in!

1 shallot, chopped

1 tablespoon olive oil

4 cups low-sodium chicken broth, no sugar added

1½ pounds cremini mushrooms, cleaned and sliced

1 teaspoon garlic powder

¼ cup chopped fresh flat leaf parsley

Salt to taste

Grated Parmesan for garnish

NUTRITIONAL DATA

Calories: 71

Total Fat: 3g

Saturated Fat: 0g

Trans Fat: 0g

Cholesterol: 3mg

Sodium: 86mg

Carbohydrates: 8g

Dietary Fiber: 1g

Sugars: 3g

Protein: 4g

Using a medium soup pot, sauté the shallot in the olive oil until it becomes a bit translucent. Pour in the chicken broth, and add the mushrooms, garlic powder, and parsley. Cook at a gentle boil until the mushrooms are wilted. Add salt to taste, and serve topped with a small amount of Parmesan cheese.

Note: The flavors of this soup develop a bit more with time. Allowing the soup to sit and cool for an hour or so will make for a tastier soup.

Mushroom and Spinach Soup

Mushroom and Spinach Soup

YIELD: 12 SERVINGS   SERVING SIZE: 1 CUP

This delicious, low-calorie, low-fat, and low-cholesterol soup will give you about 19% of your recommended daily vitamin A. Included with that are vitamins C and B6. Not too bad for 58 calories per cup!

8 cups low-sodium chicken broth, no sugar added
6 sodium-free chicken bouillon cubes
2¼ pounds baby bella or cremini mushrooms
4 cups fresh spinach
2 tablespoons low-sodium soy sauce
2 teaspoons onion powder
2 teaspoons garlic powder

Combine all ingredients in a large pot, and bring to a boil. Reduce to a simmer. Stir frequently until the mushrooms are soft and cooked through.

NUTRITIONAL DATA
Calories: 58
Total Fat: 1g
Saturated Fat: 1g
Trans Fat: 0g
Cholesterol: 3mg
Sodium: 244mg
Carbohydrates: 8g
Dietary Fiber: 1g
Sugars: 3g
Protein: 4g

German Cabbage and Apple Soup

YIELD: 7 SERVINGS   SERVING SIZE: 1 CUP

Turkey or lean beef meatballs make an excellent addition to this dish.

1 small head cabbage, cored and sliced
1 small apple, peeled, cored, and chopped
6 cups low-sodium chicken broth, no sugar added
¼ cup caraway seeds
¼ cup chopped fresh parsley
1 vegetable bouillon cube (we used Rapunzel brand)

Bring all ingredients to a boil, reduce to a simmer, and cook until cabbage is cooked through.

NUTRITIONAL DATA
Calories: 74
Total Fat: 2g
Saturated Fat: 0g
Trans Fat: 0g
Cholesterol: 4mg
Sodium: 156mg
Carbohydrates: 13g
Dietary Fiber: 5g
Sugars: 6g
Protein: 3g

Lemon Asparagus Soup

YIELD: 7 SERVINGS   SERVING SIZE: 1 CUP

This low-calorie soup is sure to please with fabulous flavor and a plentiful supply of vitamins A, C, and K, folate, and iron. Enjoy by itself as a light lunch, or as a first course to dinner.

5 cups sliced asparagus

4 cups low-sodium vegetable broth, no sugar added

2 cubes vegetable bouillon (we used Rapunzel brand)

¼ cup fresh lemon juice

½ cup chopped fresh parsley

1 teaspoon dill

½ teaspoon ground black pepper

¼ cup plain, nonfat Greek-style yogurt

Salt to taste

Combine asparagus, broth, bouillon, lemon juice, parsley, dill, and pepper in a medium soup pot. Bring to a boil, and reduce to a simmer. Cook until the asparagus is done to your liking. Remove from heat, cool slightly, and stir in yogurt. Add salt to taste, and serve.

> NUTRITIONAL DATA
> Sodium content will vary widely based on broth used.
>
> Calories: 45
> Total Fat: 1g
> Saturated Fat: 1g
> Trans Fat: 0g
> Cholesterol: 0mg
> Sodium: 270mg
> Carbohydrates: 7g
> Dietary Fiber: 2g
> Sugars: 3g
> Protein: 4g

Tomato Basil Soup

YIELD: 5 SERVINGS   SERVING SIZE: 1 CUP

Roasted tomatoes have up to eight times the amount of the powerful antioxidant lycopene than uncooked tomatoes.

1 pound fresh tomatoes

3 tablespoons extra virgin olive oil, divided

1 carrot, diced

1 stalk celery, diced

2 garlic cloves, minced

2 medium shallots, chopped

¼ cup chopped fresh basil (lemon basil is recommended)

Dash of cayenne pepper

Bay leaf

Sea salt and freshly ground pepper to taste

2 cups fat-free, low-sodium vegetable broth

Preheat oven to 400°.

Slice tomatoes in half; place on foil-lined cookie sheet. Drizzle 1 tablespoon of oil over tomatoes. Slightly fold the edges of the foil in, toward the tomatoes, to capture any juice. In the meantime, in a small skillet on medium-low heat, sauté diced carrot and celery in the remaining 2 tablespoons of oil until tender, 10–15 minutes. Add garlic and shallots; turn heat to low and continue to sauté another 5 minutes.

Remove tomatoes from the oven, allow to cool 15 minutes or until they are cool enough to handle. Peel the tomatoes; the peeling should easily slide off. Discard peelings. If desired, push tomatoes through a sieve to remove any seeds. (It's not necessary to remove seeds, but rather a personal preference. I prefer to leave the seeds.)

Add all ingredients to a food processor, or use an emulsion blender to purée.

Add tomato purée and broth to medium pot, bring to a boil; reduce heat to a low simmer and cook 15–20 minutes. If a thicker soup is preferred, combine 1 tablespoon cornstarch and 1 tablespoon cold broth or water; add to soup, stir, and allow to simmer a few more minutes until thickened. Remove bay leaf and serve.

NUTRITIONAL DATA

Calories: 125	Sodium: 78mg
Total Fat: 9g	Carbohydrates: 12g
Saturated Fat: 1g	Dietary Fiber: 2g
Trans Fat: 0g	Sugars: 3g
Cholesterol: 0mg	Protein: 2g

Carrot and Parsnip Soup

YIELD: 6 SERVINGS   SERVING SIZE: 1 CUP

Whether on a cold winter's day, or a hot summer's night, this superfood soup is delicious anytime of the year. You can also enjoy this soup knowing that there are many health benefits, such as containing vitamin C, fiber, and calcium. I think of beautiful, glowing skin when eating this hearty soup, thanks to its hefty amount of vitamin A.

½ pound carrots, peeled, sliced into ½-inch pieces

½ pound parsnips, peeled, sliced into ½-inch pieces

1 medium russet potato, peeled, cut into ½-inch cubes

1 tablespoon extra virgin olive oil

2 garlic cloves, minced

1 small sweet onion, diced

3 cups fat-free, low-sodium vegetable broth

½ teaspoon black pepper

1 tablespoon chopped fresh parsley

¼ teaspoon cayenne pepper

Salt to taste

3 cups low-sodium vegetable broth

¾ cup milk

Steam carrots, parsnips, and potato until tender. If using a double boiler with steamer insert, add 2–3 inches of water to the bottom pot; add vegetables to the insert; cover. Heat water to boiling; reduce heat to low and steam until tender. Cool 15 minutes before puréeing.

While vegetables are steaming, add oil to a small skillet, heat to medium-low, and add garlic and onion; cook until tender, approximately 5 minutes. Remove from heat; add onion, garlic, and cooled vegetables to a food processor, or use an immersion blender; pulse until puréed.

Add purée to a large pot along with spices and broth. Bring to a boil on medium heat, reduce to a simmer, and continue cooking 15 minutes. Add milk, and continue to cook until hot, approximately 5 minutes.

NUTRITIONAL DATA

Calories: 95	Sodium: 92mg
Total Fat: 2g	Carbohydrates: 17g
Saturated Fat: 0g	Dietary Fiber: 3g
Trans Fat: 0g	Sugars: 5g
Cholesterol: 1mg	Protein: 2g

Superfood Soup Supreme

YIELD: 8 SERVINGS   **SERVING SIZE: 1 CUP**

Five root vegetables make this recipe ultra-superfood enriched. Whether a fan of beets or not, you'll love the taste these five vegetables create when coming together as one thick, rich and creamy soup.

1 beet, peeled, coarsely chopped

1 large potato, peeled, coarsely chopped

1 large carrot, peeled, sliced into 1-inch pieces

1 turnip, peeled, coarsely chopped

½ celery root, peeled, coarsely chopped

2 tablespoons extra virgin olive oil

2 shallots, diced

2 garlic cloves, diced

1 teaspoon black pepper

Sea or kosher salt to taste

3 cups fat-free, low-sodium vegetable broth

2 teaspoons white balsamic vinegar

1 tablespoon chopped fresh dill

1 cup 2% milk

½ cup plain, nonfat Greek-style yogurt

Steam the beet, potato, carrot, turnip, and celery root until very tender, about 30 minutes.

While vegetables are steaming, add oil to a small skillet, and heat to medium-low; add shallots and garlic; cook until tender, approximately 6 minutes. Remove from heat; add shallots, garlic, and cooled vegetables to a food processor, or use an immersion blender; pulse until puréed.

NUTRITIONAL DATA	
Calories: 132	Sodium: 88mg
Total Fat: 4g	Carbohydrates: 22g
Saturated Fat: 1g	Dietary Fiber: 2g
Trans Fat: 0g	Sugars: 4g
Cholesterol: 2mg	Protein: 4g

Return vegetable purée to a large saucepan; add remaining ingredients, stir, and bring to a simmer. Cook 15 minutes, or until heated through. Garnish with additional dill. This soup can be served hot or cold.

Sweet Potato and Apple Dessert Soup

YIELD: 7 SERVINGS   SERVING SIZE: 1 CUP

Surprise your dinner guests with this unique blend of sweet potatoes and tart Granny Smith apples, along with a little rum extract . . . unusually delicious! This soup is more than just a sweet treat; it may also help in the fight against certain types of cancer.

2½ cups chopped sweet potatoes, peeled

2 Granny Smith apples, cored and peeled

½ teaspoon cinnamon

¼ teaspoon nutmeg

Dash of allspice

Pinch of sea salt

1½ cups apple juice, unsweetened

½ cup 100% orange juice

1 teaspoon 100% pure rum extract

2 teaspoons honey

¼ cup plain, nonfat Greek-style yogurt

NUTRITIONAL DATA	
Calories: 148	Sodium: 54mg
Total Fat: 0g	Carbohydrates: 34g
Saturated Fat: 0g	Dietary Fiber: 4g
Trans Fat: 0g	Sugars: 18g
Cholesterol: 0mg	Protein: 3g

Steam sweet potatoes and apples. If using a double boiler with steamer insert, add 2–3 inches of water to the bottom pot; add vegetables to the insert; cover. Heat water to boiling, reduce heat to low, and steam until tender, about 25 minutes. Cool 15 minutes before puréeing.

Purée cooled sweet potatoes and apples by using either a food processor or an immersion blender. Add potatoes and apples to a medium saucepan, along with the spices, juices, rum extract, and honey; stir to combine. Heat on medium-low for about 15 minutes, or until heated through. Add yogurt, stir, and heat an additional 2–3 minutes.

Garnish with a dash of cinnamon or nutmeg.

Vegetable Stew, Featuring Sweet Potatoes

YIELD: 7 SERVINGS   SERVING SIZE: 1 CUP

Enjoy this hearty superfoods stew year-round. This stew is an excellent source of vitamin A, dietary fiber, and manganese.

1 tablespoon extra virgin olive oil
1 small red onion, coarsely chopped
1 garlic clove, minced
2 large sweet potatoes, peeled, coarsely chopped into 1-inch cubes
1 (14½-ounce) can diced tomatoes
1 cup fresh or frozen green peas
½ cup diced red bell peppers
2 cups fat-free, low-sodium chicken stock
1 bay leaf
1 teaspoon paprika
¼ teaspoon allspice
¼ teaspoon black pepper
Sea salt to taste

NUTRITIONAL DATA

Calories: 137	Sodium: 119mg
Total Fat: 3g	Carbohydrates: 22g
Saturated Fat: 1g	Dietary Fiber: 5g
Trans Fat: 0g	Sugars: 7g
Cholesterol: 2mg	Protein: 6g

Add oil to a large pot, turn to medium-low heat, and sauté onion and garlic until tender, about 5 minutes. Add remaining ingredients; stir to combine. Cover, bring to a boil, reduce heat to a simmer, and continue cooking for 1 hour. Stir occasionally to prevent sticking. Remove bay leaf, and serve.

3-Bean Habanero Turkey Chili

3-Bean Habanero Turkey Chili

YIELD: 10 SERVINGS   SERVING SIZE: 1 CUP

Dried beans are low in fat, high in protein, and heart healthy.

1 pound lean ground turkey
1 tablespoon olive oil
1 onion, diced
2 garlic cloves, minced
2 (15-ounce) cans Tri-beans with dark red kidney, black, and pinto beans, drained
1 (10-ounce) can diced tomatoes with habaneros
1 (6-ounce) can tomato paste
1 (4½-ounce) can diced green chiles with liquid
2 tablespoons ground chili powder
½ teaspoon black pepper
1 teaspoon crushed red pepper (optional)
Salt to taste
2 cups water

NUTRITIONAL DATA
Calories: 272
Total Fat: 7g
Saturated Fat: 1g
Trans Fat: 0g
Cholesterol: 31mg
Sodium: 183mg
Carbohydrates: 36g
Dietary Fiber: 13g
Sugars: 6g
Protein: 19g

In a large skillet, add ground turkey, and cook over medium heat. With a fork or large spoon, break up turkey into small pieces; continue cooking until it loses its pink color. Add cooked turkey to a large pot or Dutch oven.

In a small skillet, add oil, and over medium-low heat, sauté onion and garlic until tender, about 5 minutes.

Add sautéed onion, garlic, and all other ingredients to pot or Dutch oven. Cover, and bring to boil over medium-high heat; reduce heat, and simmer 1 hour. Remove lid, and continue cooking 30 minutes, or until chili has thickened.

White Bean Chicken Chili with Swiss Chard

YIELD: 8 SERVINGS   SERVING SIZE: 1 CUP

When cooking with chard, leave the brightly colored stalks in place for an even tastier, healthier dish. This superfood recipe is a good source of dietary fiber, and is high in protein, and vitamins A, C, and K.

1 tablespoon extra virgin olive oil

2 garlic cloves, minced

1 sweet onion, diced

2 halved skinless chicken breast fillets, cut into 1-inch chunks

1 (10-ounce) can petit diced tomatoes with liquid

2 tablespoons tomato paste

2 cups fat-free, low-sodium chicken broth

2 teaspoons chili powder

1 teaspoon dried oregano

¼ teaspoon crushed red pepper flakes

1 tablespoon chopped fresh cilantro

2 (15½-ounce) cans cannellini beans, drained and rinsed

¼ cup plain, nonfat Greek-style yogurt

2 cups chopped Swiss chard, with stalks

Yogurt and cilantro for garnish

NUTRITIONAL DATA

Calories: 142	Sodium: 454mg
Total Fat: 3g	Carbohydrates: 9g
Saturated Fat: 1g	Dietary Fiber: 6g
Trans Fat: 0g	Sugars: 4g
Cholesterol: 15mg	Protein: 12g

In a large saucepan, add oil, and heat to medium-low; add garlic and onion, and cook until tender, about 5 minutes. Add cubed chicken, and continue cooking until chicken is lightly browned, but not cooked through completely.

Add the remaining ingredients to saucepan, except yogurt and Swiss chard. Bring chili to a boil, reduce heat to a simmer, and cook 45 minutes, or until chicken is cooked through. Add yogurt and Swiss chard, stir, and continue cooking 15 minutes. Garnish with additional dollop of yogurt and fresh cilantro, if desired.

Salads

Freshwater Trout with Spring Mix and Grapefruit

Freshwater Trout
with Spring Mix and Grapefruit

YIELD: 4 SERVINGS   SERVING SIZE: ¼ OF RECIPE

Freshwater trout is a very good source of protein and vitamins C, K, and B12.

12 almonds, with skins, cut in half
2 (4-ounce) freshwater rainbow trout fillets
1 tablespoon extra virgin olive oil
2 cups spring mix
2 cups baby spinach
1 small red onion, thinly sliced
1 grapefruit, cut into segments
1 tablespoon capers, drained
Sea salt and black pepper to taste

> ### NUTRITIONAL DATA
> Calories: 224
> Total Fat: 12g
> Saturated Fat: 4g
> Trans Fat: 0g
> Cholesterol: 49mg
> Sodium: 189mg
> Carbohydrates: 12g
> Dietary Fiber: 4g
> Sugars: 3g
> Protein: 18g

Preheat oven to 325°. Toast almonds on a cookie sheet for 10 minutes, then allow to cool at room temperature.

Preheat oven to broil.

Line rimmed cookie sheet with nonstick foil; place trout on sheet, and drizzle with oil. Place sheet 4–5 inches from broiler, and cook 2–3 minutes on each side, or until fillets easily flake and are cooked through.

Add remaining ingredients in a large serving bowl; flake fillets, and toss with salad mix.

DRESSING:
2 tablespoons extra virgin olive oil
1 tablespoon lemon juice

Combine olive oil and lemon juice; drizzle over salad, toss, and serve.

Napa Chicken Salad

YIELD: 4 SERVINGS   SERVING SIZE: 1½ CUPS

Cabbage is packed with flavor, and it is rich in antioxidants. Vitamins A, C, and K and niacin make this an essential superfood.

2 tablespoons toasted sesame seeds

1 tablespoon canola oil

1 tablespoon sesame oil

2 chicken breast fillets, cut into ½-inch cubes (free-range is best)

3 cups shredded napa cabbage

2 cups chopped romaine lettuce

1 carrot, peeled, julienned

Preheat oven to 325°.

Place sesame seeds in a small oven-safe dish; roast 10 minutes or until lightly toasted.

In a medium skillet, add canola and sesame oil; turn heat to medium-high, and cook chicken until cooked through and crispy, approximately 10 minutes.

NUTRITIONAL DATA	
Calories: 259	Sodium: 193mg
Total Fat: 15g	Carbohydrates: 16g
Saturated Fat: 2g	Dietary Fiber: 3g
Trans Fat: 0g	Sugars: 11g
Cholesterol: 37mg	Protein: 16g

DRESSING:

2 tablespoon honey

2 teaspoons Dijon mustard

1 tablespoon lite soy sauce, low sodium

1 tablespoon rice wine vinegar

1 tablespoon freshly squeezed lemon juice

In the meantime, combine honey and mustard, and stir until smooth. Add the remaining Dressing ingredients; stir.

Combine cooked chicken, cabbage, lettuce, carrots, and sesame seeds in a large serving bowl. Drizzle on Dressing, more or less to taste, and toss to combine.

Garnish salad with a few additional sesame seeds.

Spring Mix and Strawberry Salad

YIELD: 4 SERVINGS   SERVING SIZE: 2 CUPS

Spring is in the air with this superfoods' life-enhancing magnesium. Also, it is a great source of dietary fiber, calcium, phosphorus, potassium, folate, and vitamins A, C, and K.

4 cups spring mix salad (spinach, arugula, and baby romaine)

2 cups romaine heart lettuce, torn into bite-size pieces

1 (11-ounce) can Mandarin oranges in natural juices, drained

1 cup sliced fresh strawberries

1 small red onion, sliced into thin rings

½ cup blue cheese crumbles

Candied Pecans for garnish (page 41) (optional)

> **NUTRITIONAL DATA**
> Calories: 109
> Total Fat: 5g
> Saturated Fat: 3g
> Trans Fat: 0g
> Cholesterol: 10mg
> Sodium: 217mg
> Carbohydrates: 13g
> Dietary Fiber: 3g
> Sugars: 9g
> Protein: 6g

Combine all the above ingredients in a large salad bowl; drizzle with ½ cup White Balsamic Vinaigrette, and toss to combine.

If desired, garnish with Candied Pecans (page 41).

WHITE BALSAMIC VINAIGRETTE:

YIELD: 4 SERVINGS   SERVING SIZE: 2 TABLESPOONS

¼ cup white balsamic vinegar

¼ cup extra virgin olive oil

¼ teaspoon black pepper

Salt to taste

½ teaspoon dried oregano

> **NUTRITIONAL DATA**
> Calories: 240
> Total Fat: 14g
> Saturated Fat: 2g
> Trans Fat: 0g
> Cholesterol: 0mg
> Sodium: 6mg
> Carbohydrates: 4g
> Dietary Fiber: 0g
> Sugars: 3g
> Protein: 0g

Add all ingredients to a blender, and blend until combined. Use immediately, or store in a glass jar with lid until ready to use.

Mediterranean Garden Salad

YIELD: 4 SERVINGS   SERVING SIZE: 1½ CUPS

This amazing recipe is not only low in saturated fat, sodium, and cholesterol, but it is also an excellent source of dietary fiber, riboflavin, potassium, copper, folate, manganese, and vitamins A, B6, C, and K.

4 cups torn romaine heart leaves
1 sweet (organic) apple with peeling, cubed (Gala was used in this recipe)
1 cup sliced white mushrooms
1 medium red bell pepper, sliced julienne style
6 baby carrots, sliced julienne style
1 small zucchini, sliced julienne style
¼ cup raw pine nuts
Salt and pepper to taste

NUTRITIONAL DATA
Calories: 111
Total Fat: 6g
Saturated Fat: 0g
Trans Fat: 0g
Cholesterol: 0mg
Sodium: 21mg
Carbohydrates: 14g
Dietary Fiber: 4g
Sugars: 8g
Protein: 3g

Combine all the ingredients in a large salad bowl. Drizzle salad with Pomegranate-Ginger Vinaigrette, and toss to combine. Add additional pine nuts for garnish.

POMEGRANATE-GINGER VINAIGRETTE:

YIELD: 4 SERVINGS   SERVING SIZE: 2 TABLESPOONS

This heart-healthy vinaigrette is rich with omega-3 fatty acids.

2 teaspoons honey
¼ cup extra virgin olive oil
2 tablespoons red wine vinegar
3 tablespoons 100% pure pomegranate juice, no sugar added
½ teaspoon ground ginger
⅛ teaspoon black pepper

NUTRITIONAL DATA
Calories: 263
Total Fat: 14g
Saturated Fat: 2g
Trans Fat: 0g
Cholesterol: 0mg
Sodium: 2mg
Carbohydrates: 6g
Dietary Fiber: 0g
Sugars: 5g
Protein: 3g

Add all ingredients to a blender, and blend until combined. Pour vinaigrette into a glass jar with lid, and refrigerate until ready to use.

Citrus Spinach Salad

YIELD: 2 SERVINGS   SERVING SIZE: ½ THE RECIPE

This incredibly light and refreshing salad will fill you up and keep you satisfied. It's the perfect summer salad!

2 cups raw spinach

1 medium orange, peeled and chopped

2 tablespoons dried cranberries

¼ cup chopped walnuts

Assemble all salad ingredients in a medium mixing bowl.

NUTRITIONAL DATA	
Calories: 210	Sodium: 25mg
Total Fat: 12g	Carbohydrates: 26g
Saturated Fat: 1g	Dietary Fiber: 4g
Trans Fat: 0g	Sugars: 19g
Cholesterol: 0mg	Protein: 4g

LEMON BASIL DRESSING:

2 tablespoons chopped fresh basil

1 teaspoon lightly flavored vegetable oil such as safflower

1 tablespoon lemon juice

1 teaspoon honey

In a small mixing bowl, whisk together the Dressing ingredients, and pour over the salad. Mix well, and serve.

Garden Shades of Red

Garden Shades of Red

YIELD: 4 SERVINGS   SERVING SIZE: 1½ CUPS

Here is a salad that's not only delicious and full of antioxidant qualities, but will easily grace any dinner table with its beauty. The deepest red in this garden salad is likely the beets. These red beauties have less sugar if bought fresh, which make them lower in calories than if purchased in a can.

1 head radicchio, coarsely chopped

2 cups torn red romaine lettuce

1 small red bell pepper, julienne sliced

1 medium red onion, sliced into thin rings, then cut in half

1 cup seedless red grapes, sliced in half lengthwise

1 cup grape tomatoes

2 Roasted Red Beets, sliced (page 102)

Red kale for garnish

NUTRITIONAL DATA
Calories: 98
Total Fat: 1g
Saturated Fat: 0g
Trans Fat: 0g
Cholesterol: 0mg
Sodium: 45mg
Carbohydrates: 23g
Dietary Fiber: 4g
Sugars: 15g
Protein: 3g

In a large salad bowl, combine the first 6 ingredients; drizzle with Black Cherry Vinaigrette, and toss to combine; add beets on top, and garnish with red kale.

BLACK CHERRY VINAIGRETTE:

YIELD: 8 SERVINGS   SERVING SIZE: 2 TABLESPOONS

2 teaspoons honey

¼ cup extra virgin olive oil

2 tablespoons red wine vinegar

2 tablespoons plus 2 teaspoons black cherry juice, no sugar added

½ teaspoon rubbed sage

NUTRITIONAL DATA
Calories: 105
Total Fat: 14g
Saturated Fat: 2g
Trans Fat: 0g
Cholesterol: 0mg
Sodium: 1mg
Carbohydrates: 7g
Dietary Fiber: 0g
Sugars: 7g
Protein: 0g

Add all ingredients to a blender, and blend until smooth and combined. Pour vinaigrette in a glass jar with lid, and refrigerate until ready to use.

Endive with Beets and Pistachios

YIELD: 4 SERVINGS   SERVING SIZE: 1½ CUPS

4 cups endive

**2 Roasted Red Beets, sliced
(page 102)**

¼ cup pistachios

¼ cup goat cheese

Freshly ground black pepper

Salt to taste

NUTRITIONAL DATA

Calories: 123	Sodium: 102mg
Total Fat: 9g	Carbohydrates: 7g
Saturated Fat: 3g	Dietary Fiber: 3g
Trans Fat: 0g	Sugars: 3g
Cholesterol: 11mg	Protein: 6g

Place endive in a salad bowl; top with beets, pistachios, and goat cheese, and drizzle with Orange-Tarragon Vinaigrette. Season to taste.

ORANGE-TARRAGON VINAIGRETTE:

YIELD: 8 SERVINGS   SERVING SIZE: 2 TABLESPOONS

¼ cup extra virgin olive oil

**2 tablespoons white balsamic
vinegar**

**3 tablespoons freshly squeezed
orange juice**

½ teaspoon dried tarragon

**2 dashes freshly ground black
pepper**

Pinch of sea salt

NUTRITIONAL DATA

Calories: 66	Sodium: 141mg
Total Fat: 7g	Carbohydrates: 1g
Saturated Fat: 1g	Dietary Fiber: 0g
Trans Fat: 0g	Sugars: 1g
Cholesterol: 0mg	Protein: 0g

Add all the ingredients to a blender, and blend until combined. Refrigerate until ready to use.

Belgian Endive and Apple Salad

YIELD: 2½ SERVINGS   SERVING SIZE: 1 CUP

This incredibly nutritious salad is not only delicious, but is packed with approximately 149% of your daily vitamin A requirement. In addition, you get approximately 57% of your vitamin C requirement, 20% calcium, and 18% iron. You'll also enjoy a ton of minerals such as magnesium, potassium, zinc, copper, and an amazing amount of fiber per serving. This salad is tough to beat. (Percentages based on a 2,000-calorie diet.)

6 endive, halved and chopped
2 medium apples, chopped
1 medium pear, peeled and chopped
1 medium orange, chopped
1 tablespoon lemon juice
½ cup coarsely chopped almonds

NUTRITIONAL DATA	
Calories: 250	Sodium: 14mg
Total Fat: 8g	Carbohydrates: 42g
Saturated Fat: 2g	Dietary Fiber: 4g
Trans Fat: 0g	Sugars: 16g
Cholesterol: 0mg	Protein: 6g

Combine all salad ingredients in a large mixing bowl.

DRESSING:

1 cup plain, nonfat Greek-style yogurt
¼ cup honey

Combine the Dressing ingredients in a small mixing bowl, and pour into the salad just prior to eating. Mix well, and serve.

Note: It may be best to let everyone add their own Dressing after serving; this salad won't keep long with Dressing on it.

Heirloom Tomato Salad with Herbs

YIELD: 5 SERVINGS   SERVING SIZE: 1 CUP

The wonderful taste of heirloom tomatoes is undeniable. The same can be said about the health benefits of this superfood. Tomatoes are packed with lycopene, which may help lower the risk of prostate, breast, and lung cancer.

2 pounds heirloom tomatoes, variety of shapes and colors

2 cups chopped arugula

1 small Vidalia or sweet onion, thinly sliced

1 coarsely chopped tablespoon each: fresh basil, mint, oregano, and thyme

Sea salt and black pepper to taste

2 tablespoons extra virgin olive oil

2 tablespoons white balsamic vinegar

2 tablespoons feta cheese crumbles

Slice tomatoes, and place in a serving dish over arugula and onion. Sprinkle fresh herbs over tomatoes; salt and pepper to taste. Drizzle oil and vinegar over tomatoes; add feta crumbles.

NUTRITIONAL DATA

Calories: 105
Total Fat: 6g
Saturated Fat: 1g
Trans Fat: 0g
Cholesterol: 1mg
Sodium: 90mg
Carbohydrates: 12g
Dietary Fiber: 3g
Sugars: 7g
Protein: 3g

Peanut Cabbage Salad

YIELD: 7 SERVINGS   SERVING SIZE: 1 CUP

You'll be getting a good dose of vitamins A, C, and K with this wonderfully flavorful salad. Full of crunch, this dish will fill you up and keep you satisfied.

1 cup grated carrots

5 cups finely chopped red cabbage (about ½ of a medium head)

1 cup raisins

Combine all salad ingredients in a large mixing bowl.

NUTRITIONAL DATA
Data may vary based on peanut butter used.

Calories: 146	Sodium: 160mg
Total Fat: 5g	Carbohydrates: 25g
Saturated Fat: 1g	Dietary Fiber: 3g
Trans Fat: 0g	Sugars: 16g
Cholesterol: 0mg	Protein: 4g

DRESSING:

½ cup chicken broth

1 tablespoon low-sodium soy sauce

¼ cup creamy peanut butter, no sugar added

Whisk together all Dressing ingredients in a small mixing bowl, and pour over salad. Mix well, and serve.

Creamy Cabbage and Bok Choy Slaw

YIELD: 6 SERVINGS   SERVING SIZE: ⅔ CUP

Here's an old standard at any summertime barbecue; but this side just happens to be packed with superfood goodness. There is evidence in the scientific community to indicate a connection between cruciferous vegetables, such as cabbage, and a lower risk of premenopausal breast cancer.

⅓ cup mayonnaise, no added sweeteners (Duke's is a favorite for this recipe)

2 tablespoons low-fat buttermilk

1 tablespoon low-fat milk

2 tablespoons 100% pure maple syrup

2 tablespoons white balsamic or apple cider vinegar

½ head cabbage, chopped

1 stalk bok choy, leaves removed and chopped

2 tablespoons diced red bell pepper

1 small carrot, peeled and shredded

Salt and pepper to taste

NUTRITIONAL DATA

Calories: 88	Sodium: 116mg
Total Fat: 4g	Carbohydrates: 11g
Saturated Fat: 1g	Dietary Fiber: 2g
Trans Fat: 0g	Sugars: 8g
Cholesterol: 0mg	Protein: 1g

Add the first 5 ingredients to a blender, and blend until smooth. Place slaw dressing in a glass jar with a lid, and refrigerate until ready to use, chilling for approximately 2 hours.

Coarsely chop cabbage and bok choy; if using a food processor, add small chunks, being careful not to overpulse, as this will make it mushy. Combine in a large mixing bowl, the cabbage, bok choy, bell pepper, and carrot. Season with salt and pepper to taste.

Add slaw dressing to cabbage mix; stir to combine, cover, and refrigerate until ready to eat.

Tip: Cole slaw is always best eaten on the same day as prepared.

Carrot and Cherry Tomato Egg Salad

YIELD: 4½ SERVINGS   SERVING SIZE: 1 CUP

20 large, hard-boiled egg whites, chopped

1 cup plain, nonfat Greek-style yogurt

1 teaspoon yellow mustard

½ teaspoon paprika

½ teaspoon garlic powder

2 teaspoons onion powder

1 teaspoon dill

1 cup finely grated carrots

1 cup halved cherry tomatoes

Salt to taste

NUTRITIONAL DATA

Calories: 124	Sodium: 294mg
Total Fat: 0g	Carbohydrates: 8g
Saturated Fat: 0g	Dietary Fiber: 2g
Trans Fat: 0g	Sugars: 6g
Cholesterol: 0mg	Protein: 22g

Mix all together, and serve.

Note: You can use whole eggs, but the cholesterol takes a huge leap. Simply sub 1 yolk for 2 egg whites.

Carrot Pistachio Salad with Ginger

YIELD: 3½ SERVINGS   SERVING SIZE: 1 CUP

Get some vitamins A and C into your day with this lovely and satisfying salad. It pairs nicely with almost any meat dish and is a wonderful way to add some fiber to your eating plan.

3 cups grated carrots

½ cup finely chopped shelled pistachio nutmeats (unsalted)

¼- to ½-inch slice ginger to taste, minced

Juice of 1 lemon

Salt to taste

NUTRITIONAL DATA

Calories: 164	Sodium: 78mg
Total Fat: 8g	Carbohydrates: 22g
Saturated Fat: 2g	Dietary Fiber: 6g
Trans Fat: 0g	Sugars: 8g
Cholesterol: 0mg	Protein: 6g

Combine everything together in a bowl, and serve.

Rainbow Salad

Rainbow Salad

YIELD: 4 SERVINGS   SERVING SIZE: 1 CUP

Colors of the rainbow foods, or superfoods, have long been thought to have disease-preventing properties. Bell peppers are thought to help in the prevention of heart disease, strokes, and blood clots.

1 red bell pepper, cut into strips
1 yellow bell pepper, cut into strips
1 green bell pepper, cut into strips
6 radishes, thinly sliced
1 small red onion, quartered, thinly sliced
1 small cucumber, cut in half and thinly sliced
¼ cup blue cheese crumbles (optional)

Combine all ingredients in a salad bowl, toss to combine, drizzle with Honey-Lemon Dressing, and top with blue cheese crumbles, if desired.

NUTRITIONAL DATA
Calories: 94
Total Fat: 4g
Saturated Fat: 2g
Trans Fat: 0g
Cholesterol: 8mg
Sodium: 166mg
Carbohydrates: 12g
Dietary Fiber: 3g
Sugars: 5g
Protein: 4g

HONEY-LEMON DRESSING:

YIELD: 4 SERVINGS   SERVING SIZE: ¼ OF RECIPE

2 tablespoons honey
2 tablespoons lemon juice
2 tablespoons extra virgin olive oil
¼ teaspoon dried oregano
⅛ teaspoon freshly ground black pepper
Salt to taste

Combine ingredients in blender, and blend until smooth. Refrigerate until ready to use.

NUTRITIONAL DATA
Calories: 93
Total Fat: 7g
Saturated Fat: 1g
Trans Fat: 0g
Cholesterol: 0mg
Sodium: 1mg
Carbohydrates: 9g
Dietary Fiber: 0g
Sugars: 9g
Protein: 0g

Roasted Beet and Fennel Salad

YIELD: 4 SERVINGS   SERVING SIZE: 1 CUP

Beets are known for being heart healthy and having anti-aging effects. Additional benefits also include being high in dietary fiber, vitamin C, folate, potassium, as well as bone-healthy manganese. Have you had your beets today?

3 medium fresh red beets, scrubbed and dried

2 teaspoons olive oil

2 fennel bulbs, shredded

1 cup arugula

½ cup diced walnuts

¼ cup blue cheese crumbles

¼ teaspoon freshly ground black pepper

Salt to taste

NUTRITIONAL DATA	
Calories: 210	Sodium: 228mg
Total Fat: 15g	Carbohydrates: 17g
Saturated Fat: 3g	Dietary Fiber: 6g
Trans Fat: 0g	Sugars: 5g
Cholesterol: 6mg	Protein: 7g

To roast beets, preheat oven to 350°. Brush beets with oil; wrap individually in foil, place on a cookie sheet, and bake approximately 1 hour, or until tender. Allow beets to cool at room temperature, then peel the thin outer skin, and cut into ¼-inch slices. Store beets in an airtight container in the refrigerator until ready to use.

Layer salad ingredients by placing beets on a serving platter; add fennel, arugula, walnuts, and blue cheese; top off with freshly ground black pepper and salt. Drizzle with Lemon-Oil Dressing.

LEMON-OIL DRESSING:

YIELD: 4 SERVINGS   SERVING SIZE: 1 TABLESPOON

¼ cup freshly squeezed lemon juice

¼ cup extra virgin olive oil

Combine lemon juice and oil in a blender, and blend until smooth. Store in a glass decanter with top; refrigerate until ready to use.

NUTRITIONAL DATA	
Calories: 123	Sodium: 0mg
Total Fat: 14g	Carbohydrates: 1g
Saturated Fat: 2g	Dietary Fiber: 0g
Trans Fat: 0g	Sugars: 0g
Cholesterol: 0mg	Protein: 0g

4-Bean Salad

YIELD: 6½ SERVINGS   SERVING SIZE: 1 CUP

Get your fiber for the day with this delicious salad. It makes a wonderful companion dish to almost any type of meat.

1½ cups cooked black beans
1½ cups cooked pinto beans
1½ cups cooked cannellini beans
1½ cups cooked kidney beans
1 cup grated carrots
**½ medium red bell pepper, chopped
  fine**

NUTRITIONAL DATA	
Calories: 366	Sodium: 18mg
Total Fat: 2g	Carbohydrates: 68g
Saturated Fat: 0g	Dietary Fiber: 20g
Trans Fat: 0g	Sugars: 2g
Cholesterol: 0mg	Protein: 22g

Combine all ingredients in a large mixing bowl.

DRESSING:

2 tablespoons rice vinegar
1 teaspoon honey
1 teaspoon dried tarragon
½ teaspoon onion powder
½ teaspoon garlic powder
Salt to taste

In a small mixing bowl, whisk together the Dressing ingredients, and pour over the beans. Mix well, and serve.

Note: If using canned beans, use the 15-ounce can . . . and be sure there is no added sugar. Also, the sodium content can skyrocket in canned goods. Look for low- or no-sodium beans.

Black Bean and Brown Rice Salad

YIELD: 5 SERVINGS   SERVING SIZE: 1 CUP

1½ cups home-cooked black beans, or 1 (15-ounce) can black beans, no sugar added

3 cups cooked and cooled brown rice, cooked to package directions

1½ cups finely grated raw zucchini

2 garlic cloves, chopped

1 tablespoon olive oil

½ cup diced red onion

½ cup grated Parmesan cheese

Mix all ingredients together in a large mixing bowl, and serve.

NUTRITIONAL DATA
Calories: 292
Total Fat: 7g
Saturated Fat: 2g
Trans Fat: 0g
Cholesterol: 9mg
Sodium: 163mg
Carbohydrates: 46g
Dietary Fiber: 6g
Sugars: 3g
Protein: 12g

Broccoli and Rice Parmesan Salad

YIELD: 7 SERVINGS   SERVING SIZE: 1 CUP

This dish is very filling and can easily accommodate the addition of almost any lean meat you care to enjoy with it. It is excellent with added chunks of baked chicken breast.

3 garlic cloves, chopped fine
1 tablespoon olive oil
7 cups chopped raw broccoli
2 tablespoons fresh chopped basil
1 teaspoon dried tarragon
2 cups cooked brown rice
¾ cup grated Parmesan cheese
Salt to taste

In a large frying pan, sauté the garlic in the olive oil for 1–2 minutes, then add the broccoli. Cook, stirring frequently, for 5–10 minutes, or until the broccoli is al dente. Add remaining ingredients, and continue stirring to combine well. Cool slightly, and serve.

NUTRITIONAL DATA
Calories: 162
Total Fat: 6g
Saturated Fat: 2g
Trans Fat: 0g
Cholesterol: 9mg
Sodium: 195mg
Carbohydrates: 21g
Dietary Fiber: 3g
Sugars: 2g
Protein: 8g

Tropical Brown Rice Salad

YIELD: 9 CUPS   SERVING SIZE: 1 CUP

1 cup cooked brown rice
1 cup sliced bananas
½ cup canned pineapple chunks, juice reserved, drained, no sugar added (fresh works, too, but reserve some juice)
¼ cup chopped or slivered almonds
¼ cup lite coconut milk
1 tablespoon pineapple juice drained from chunks
1 teaspoon honey
Scant pinch salt

NUTRITIONAL DATA
Calories: 175
Total Fat: 4g
Saturated Fat: 0g
Trans Fat: 0g
Cholesterol: 0mg
Sodium: 84mg
Carbohydrates: 32g
Dietary Fiber: 13g
Sugars: 17g
Protein: 8g

Combine all ingredients in a medium mixing bowl, and serve.

Roasted Hazelnut, Plum, and Strawberry Salad

Super Fruit Salad

YIELD: 5 SERVINGS   SERVING SIZE: 1 CUP

We thought about calling this the vitamin C salad. At about 67% of your daily recommended allowance (based on a 2,000-calorie diet), this is a delicious and lightly filling way to get this important vitamin.

1 cup grated apple
1 cup chopped mango
1 cup chopped pineapple
1 cup chopped blueberries
1 cup chopped strawberries
2 tablespoons flax seeds
Juice of ½ lemon

> **NUTRITIONAL DATA**
> Calories: 100   Sodium: 3mg
> Total Fat: 2g   Carbohydrates: 21g
> Saturated Fat: 0g   Dietary Fiber: 4g
> Trans Fat: 0g   Sugars: 15g
> Cholesterol: 0mg   Protein: 2g

Mix all ingredients together in a large mixing bowl, and serve.

Roasted Hazelnut, Plum, and Strawberry Salad

YIELD: 6 SERVINGS   SERVING SIZE: 1 CUP

This simple salad is truly satisfying. It's mildly sweet and packed with nutrition. It's high in good-for-you fats, and pairs nicely with baked chicken.

2 cups hazelnuts, roasted, skins rubbed off
2 cups chopped plums
2 cups chopped strawberries
2 tablespoons honey (more, if your strawberries are not very sweet)
1 teaspoon pure vanilla extract
½ teaspoon ground cinnamon

> **NUTRITIONAL DATA**
> Calories: 349   Sodium: 1mg
> Total Fat: 28g   Carbohydrates: 24g
> Saturated Fat: 2g   Dietary Fiber: 6g
> Trans Fat: 0g   Sugars: 16g
> Cholesterol: 0mg   Protein: 8g

Mix together, and serve.

Waldorf Salad with Creamy Yogurt

YIELD: 4 SERVINGS   SERVING SIZE: 1 CUP

Yogurt dressing gives a twist to this classic that has a wonderful creamy taste and the added benefits of superfood goodness. The pears in this salad are high in fiber. Eating this sweet fruit may help to lower cholesterol and reduce the risk of heart disease and diabetes.

½ cup walnut halves

½ cup plain, nonfat Greek-style yogurt

1 teaspoon lemon juice

1 teaspoon canola oil

1 tablespoon mild honey

2 Asian pears, cored, peeled, and cut into ½-inch cubes

1 cup sliced fresh strawberries

2 Honeycrisp apples, cored, with peel, and cut into ½-inch cubes

1 cup seedless grapes, sliced in half lengthwise

¼ cup raisins

Lightly roast walnut halves for 10–12 minutes at 325°. Allow to cool at room temperature.

NUTRITIONAL DATA	
Calories: 389	Sodium: 3mg
Total Fat: 6g	Carbohydrates: 77g
Saturated Fat: 1g	Dietary Fiber: 11g
Trans Fat: 0g	Sugars: 32g
Cholesterol: 0mg	Protein: 12g

In a small bowl, combine the next 4 ingredients, cover, and refrigerate until ready to use.

Combine all fruits and walnuts in a large salad bowl. Add yogurt dressing, and lightly toss to coat. Refrigerate until ready to serve. For best results, eat salad within 1–2 hours of preparing.

Vegetables and Sides

Garlic Mushroom-Stuffed Tomatoes

Garlic Mushroom-Stuffed Tomatoes

YIELD: 4 SERVINGS   SERVING SIZE: 2 HALVES

Pairs wonderfully with chicken breasts, a whole-grain side dish, and salad.

4 Roma tomatoes
½ pound brown (cremini) mushrooms, chopped
4 large garlic cloves, chopped
2 tablespoons chopped fresh parsley
1 tablespoon olive oil
¼ cup grated Parmesan cheese

Halve the tomatoes, remove and chop the insides, and set both aside. Sauté the mushrooms, garlic, and parsley in the olive oil over medium heat. The mushrooms will release a lot of liquid. When the liquid has cooked out, add the mushroom mixture to the chopped tomatoes in a mixing bowl, along with the Parmesan cheese. Mix well.

Fill the tomato halves with equal amounts of mushroom mixture. Garnish with some fresh parsley sprigs, and serve.

NUTRITIONAL DATA
Calories: 114
Total Fat: 6g
Saturated Fat: 2g
Trans Fat: 0g
Cholesterol: 6mg
Sodium: 105mg
Carbohydrates: 10g
Dietary Fiber: 1g
Sugars: 6g
Protein: 6g

Roasted Vegetable Medley

YIELD: 4 SERVINGS   SERVING SIZE: 1 CUP

Serve this side dish with meat or fish, or grab a bowl and enjoy it all by itself. To add a twist, include your favorite apple. Almost any vegetable that can be cut circular will work . . . eggplant, various squash, red potatoes . . . think colorful.

1 sweet onion, thinly sliced

3 tablespoons extra virgin olive oil

2 garlic cloves, minced

2 tablespoons chopped fresh basil

½ red bell pepper, cored, seeded, cut in strips

3 Roma tomatoes, thinly sliced

2 zucchini, thinly sliced

2 yellow squash, thinly sliced

Sea salt and black pepper to taste

¼ cup grated Parmesan cheese

NUTRITIONAL DATA	
Calories: 156	Sodium: 103mg
Total Fat: 12g	Carbohydrates: 11g
Saturated Fat: 2g	Dietary Fiber: 3g
Trans Fat: 0g	Sugars: 6g
Cholesterol: 6mg	Protein: 4g

In a medium skillet, turn heat to medium low; sauté onion in oil until caramelized, 10–12 minutes. Add garlic, and sauté 1 additional minute. Add onion and garlic to an 8x8-inch baking pan; spread to evenly distribute. Sprinkle on chopped basil.

Preheat oven to 350°. Add vegetables to a large mixing bowl, drizzle with extra virgin olive oil, and sprinkle on sea salt and black pepper to taste. Toss vegetables to coat. Place vegetables in baking pan, and alternate so the colors are varied. Lay bell pepper strips on top of vegetables between layers. Sprinkle with cheese, loosely cover with foil, and bake 30 minutes. Uncover, and bake an additional 30 minutes, or until lightly browned. Sprinkle with additional cheese, if desired. Remove from oven, and serve immediately.

Zucchini-Carrot Croquettes

YIELD: 7 SERVINGS   SERVING SIZE: 1 CROQUETTE

These easy-to-make patties have a taste similar to potato pancakes while having numerous health benefits. Enjoy this delicious side, knowing that your family is getting a wealth of nutrients.

1 medium zucchini

1 medium carrot, peeled

3 green onions, diced

1 egg white, slightly beaten

½ cup cooked green lentils, drained

¼ cup whole-wheat panko crumbs, or whole-grain bread crumbs

½ cup white whole-wheat flour, or whole-wheat or oat flour

½ teaspoon baking powder

2 tablespoons wheat germ

1 teaspoon freshly ground black pepper

Dash of cayenne pepper

Sea salt to taste

1 tablespoon canola oil

NUTRITIONAL DATA	
Calories: 142	Sodium: 52mg
Total Fat: 3g	Carbohydrates: 22g
Saturated Fat: 1g	Dietary Fiber: 5g
Trans Fat: 0g	Sugars: 2g
Cholesterol: 0mg	Protein: 7g

In a medium bowl, shred zucchini and carrot using the small hole of the shredder. Using a paper towel, press on zucchini and carrot shreddings to remove excess liquid. Add onions, egg white, and lentils; use a fork, potato masher, or food processor to mash ingredients together.

Combine dry ingredients; add to zucchini and carrot mixture. Make 7–8 patties. The mixture will be wet but holds up well when cooking. In a large skillet, add canola oil, turn to medium-low, add patties, and cook until set and browned; flip over. Cook approximately 4–5 minutes on each side. Serve immediately.

Maple Roasted Carrots

YIELD: 3 SERVINGS   SERVING SIZE: 1 CUP

Looking for a new way to serve carrots? This recipe is full of fiber, vitamins C, K, and A, potassium, and manganese. The kids will love this sweet dish, and you'll love all the fiber and vitamins they are getting!

3 tablespoons pure maple syrup
½ teaspoon cinnamon
¼ teaspoon ground ginger
Juice of 1 lemon
3 cups thinly sliced carrots

Combine first 4 ingredients, mix with carrots, and bake at 350° for approximately 45 minutes or until fully cooked. Stir at least once during roasting.

NUTRITIONAL DATA	
Calories: 108	Sodium: 86mg
Total Fat: 0g	Carbohydrates: 27g
Saturated Fat: 0g	Dietary Fiber: 4g
Trans Fat: 0g	Sugars: 18g
Cholesterol: 0mg	Protein: 1g

Brussels Sprouts with Garlic and Lemon Juice

YIELD: 4 SERVINGS   SERVING SIZE: ¼ RECIPE

This Brussels sprouts recipe is low in cholesterol and sodium, and is a good source for vitamins A, B6, and C.

1 (16-ounce) bag Brussels sprouts
1 tablespoon extra virgin olive oil
2 garlic cloves, minced
2 tablespoons chopped flat leaf parsley
Sea salt to taste
2 tablespoons goat cheese
Juice of ½ lemon

NUTRITIONAL DATA	
Calories: 148	Sodium: 67mg
Total Fat: 6g	Carbohydrates: 4g
Saturated Fat: 2	Dietary Fiber: 4g
Trans Fat: 0g	Sugars: 3g
Cholesterol: 6mg	Protein: 7g

Remove outer leaves of Brussels sprouts. In a medium skillet, add oil, and sauté garlic over medium-low heat until fragrant, about 1 minute. Add Brussels sprouts, cover, and reduce heat to low. Cook until tender, about 20 minutes.

Add parsley, sea salt, goat cheese, and lemon juice; toss to combine. Cook just until cheese softens, about 1 minute.

Tangy Lemon Asparagus

YIELD: 4 SERVINGS   SERVING SIZE: 1 CUP

This light and flavorful recipe is the perfect side to almost any main course.

1 tablespoon olive oil

4 cups sliced asparagus (about ½ inch thick)

Juice ½ lemon

¼ cup plain, nonfat Greek-style yogurt (regular, nonfat plain yogurt works, too)

¼ teaspoon onion powder

1 teaspoon dried tarragon

¼ teaspoon sea salt

NUTRITIONAL DATA	
Calories: 66	Sodium: 7mg
Total Fat: 4g	Carbohydrates: 6g
Saturated Fat: 1g	Dietary Fiber: 3g
Trans Fat: 0g	Sugars: 3g
Cholesterol: 0mg	Protein: 4g

Place the olive oil and asparagus in a disposable, food-safe plastic bag, and shake to coat the asparagus in oil.

Spread the asparagus on an ungreased cookie sheet, and bake at 350° for 15–17 minutes. When done, it should be soft with a slight crunch. Remove from oven, and allow to cool.

While the asparagus cools, mix the rest of the ingredients together in a medium mixing bowl. Then add the asparagus, and stir well to combine.

Garlic Mushroom Spinach

Garlic Mushroom Spinach

YIELD: 2½ SERVINGS   SERVING SIZE: 1 CUP

2 large garlic cloves, chopped
2 teaspoons olive oil
½ pound brown (cremini) mushrooms, sliced
6 cups fresh spinach leaves, packed

Over medium heat, sauté the garlic in the olive oil for about 1 minute or until it just barely begins to turn brown. Add the mushrooms, and cook until wilted. Stir in the spinach, and cook until wilted. Immediately remove from heat, and serve.

NUTRITIONAL DATA
Calories: 84
Total Fat: 4g
Saturated Fat: 0g
Trans Fat: 0g
Cholesterol: 0mg
Sodium: 64mg
Carbohydrates: 8g
Dietary Fiber: 2g
Sugars: 2g
Protein: 2g

Garlic Spinach with Peanut Sauce

YIELD: 2 SERVINGS   SERVING SIZE: 1 CUP

Enjoy your spinach with a delicious, creamy peanut sauce. This side dish is a wonderful way to add some vitamins E, B6, A, C, and K and even some iron, magnesium, and potassium to your meal.

2 garlic cloves, chopped
6 cups fresh spinach leaves, tightly packed
2 teaspoons olive oil
1 tablespoon peanut butter (chunky or creamy)
½ teaspoon low-sodium soy sauce
2 tablespoons low-sodium chicken broth

Sauté the garlic and spinach in the olive oil over medium heat until the spinach wilts. Remove from heat.

In a small mixing bowl, whisk together the peanut butter, soy sauce, and chicken broth. Pour the sauce over the spinach, and serve.

NUTRITIONAL DATA
Data may vary based on peanut butter used.

Calories: 123
Total Fat: 9g
Saturated Fat: 1g
Trans Fat: 0g
Cholesterol: 0mg
Sodium: 161mg
Carbohydrates: 8g
Dietary Fiber: 3g
Sugars: 1g
Protein: 5g

Spicy Potatoes and Spinach

YIELD: 3 SERVINGS   SERVING SIZE: 1 CUP

Enjoy this side dish with a baked chicken breast and a side salad for an enjoyably nutritious meal packed with folate, potassium, and vitamins B6, A, C, and K.

2 garlic cloves, chopped

1 large shallot, finely chopped (about ¼ cup)

1 tablespoon olive oil

1 medium russet potato (about 8 ounces), sliced thin (peeled, if desired)

4 cups tightly packed raw spinach

1 teaspoon red pepper flakes

¼ cup grated Parmesan cheese

Salt to taste

NUTRITIONAL DATA
Calories: 164
Total Fat: 7g
Saturated Fat: 2g
Trans Fat: 0g
Cholesterol: 7mg
Sodium: 167mg
Carbohydrates: 20g
Dietary Fiber: 3g
Sugars: 1g
Protein: 7g

In a large pan, sauté the garlic and shallot in the olive oil for about 1 minute. Add the potatoes, and stir well to coat the potatoes with the oil and garlic mix. Cover, and allow to cook over low heat for 15–20 minutes, stirring occasionally to prevent sticking to the bottom of the pan. Once the potatoes begin to get soft, stir in the spinach and pepper flakes. When the spinach wilts, stir in the Parmesan cheese, and immediately remove pan from heat. Stir to be sure cheese is evenly distributed. Salt to taste, and serve.

Super Bubble and Squeak

YIELD: 5 SERVINGS   SERVING SIZE: 1 CUP

Traditional Bubble and Squeak is made with green cabbage and white potatoes. But we decided to increase the nutrition values by using red cabbage and sweet potatoes. What we got was one very delicious and nutritious way to enjoy your veggies! Get plenty of fiber, vitamins B6, A, C, K, and potassium in just one serving of this delicious side dish.

1 large red onion, sliced thin
½ medium head red cabbage, sliced or chopped
1 medium sweet potato, peeled and sliced thin
1 tablespoon olive oil
1 teaspoon ground cumin
Splash of lemon juice
Salt to taste

Sauté onion, cabbage, and potato in oil until tender. Season with cumin, lemon juice, and salt to taste.

NUTRITIONAL DATA
Calories: 97
Total Fat: 3g
Saturated Fat: 0g
Trans Fat: 0g
Cholesterol: 0mg
Sodium: 43mg
Carbohydrates: 17g
Dietary Fiber: 3g
Sugars: 8g
Protein: 2g

Kale with Portobello Mushrooms

YIELD: 3 SERVINGS   SERVING SIZE: 1 CUP

Kale is the ultimate vegetable. And for those who love it, you'll be glad to know that one cup of kale has more than 1,300% of the recommended daily allowance of vitamin K (based on a 2,000-calorie diet), as well as plentiful amounts of vitamins B6, C, and A, and calcium, copper, and potassium.

1 tablespoon olive oil
2 garlic cloves, chopped
3 cups chopped kale (dino kale is best)
2 tablespoons lemon juice
½ teaspoon thyme
1½ pounds small portobello mushrooms, sliced
1 cup chopped tomatoes
Salt to taste
Parmesan cheese for topping (optional)

> NUTRITIONAL DATA
> Calories: 97
> Total Fat: 5g
> Saturated Fat: 1g
> Trans Fat: 0g
> Cholesterol: 0mg
> Sodium: 33mg
> Carbohydrates: 12g
> Dietary Fiber: 2g
> Sugars: 2g
> Protein: 3g

Combine first 6 ingredients in a large pan, and cook covered over low to medium heat, stirring occasionally, until the kale and mushrooms have wilted.

Just prior to turning off the heat, stir in the tomatoes. The idea is to warm them slightly without cooking them.

Salt to taste, and sprinkle with Parmesan, if desired.

Balsamic Bell Peppers with Basil and Garlic

YIELD: 4 SERVINGS   SERVING SIZE: ⅔ CUP

Eat your peppers! Orange bell peppers may help in the fight against macular degeneration; red peppers help with night vision; and yellow peppers, like their orange and red cousins, give a boost to the immune system.

1 red bell pepper
1 orange bell pepper
1 yellow bell pepper
2 tablespoons extra virgin olive oil
2 garlic cloves, minced
¼ cup diced sweet onion
1 tablespoon chopped fresh basil
¼ cup white balsamic vinegar

Cut bell peppers in half; remove stem, seeds, and ribs. Next, cut each half down the middle lengthwise. Heat oil on medium-low heat, add all ingredients to a large, nonstick skillet, and stir to combine. Cover, reduce heat to a simmer, and continue cooking 20 minutes. If desired, remove skins after peppers have cooled enough to handle. Cut peppers into ½-inch strips, place on a serving platter, and drizzle with remaining liquid in skillet.

In addition to being a delicious side dish, these colorful peppers taste great on pizza, sandwiches, pasta dishes, and more.

NUTRITIONAL DATA

Calories: 110	Sodium: 8mg
Total Fat: 7g	Carbohydrates: 10g
Saturated Fat: 1g	Dietary Fiber: 2g
Trans Fat: 0g	Sugars: 7g
Cholesterol: 20mg	Protein: 1g

Apple Cider Vinegar Sweet Potato Fries

Apple Cider Vinegar Sweet Potato Fries

YIELD: 4 SERVINGS   SERVING SIZE: ¼ OF THE RECIPE

You'll never believe there is apple cider vinegar on these fries. The vinegar helps to bring out the flavor of the sweet potatoes, and are they ever delish! Sweet potato lovers will enjoy a zero-cholesterol, high-fiber treat with plenty of vitamin B6, manganese, and vitamin A.

2 pounds sweet potatoes, peeled and cut into fries

2 teaspoons olive oil

2 tablespoons apple cider vinegar

Salt to taste

Mix everything together by hand in a large mixing bowl until the fries are well coated.

Place in a single layer on a cookie sheet, and bake at 350° for 30 minutes. (Thinner fries may not take as long.)

NUTRITIONAL DATA
Calories: 214
Total Fat: 2g
Saturated Fat: 0g
Trans Fat: 0g
Cholesterol: 0mg
Sodium: 124mg
Carbohydrates: 45g
Dietary Fiber: 7g
Sugars: 9g
Protein: 4g

Baked Broccoli Parmesan

YIELD: 6 SERVINGS   SERVING SIZE: APPROXIMATELY 1 CUP

2 heads/bunches raw broccoli, broken into smaller pieces

3 tablespoons fresh lemon juice

¼ cup grated Parmesan cheese

Olive oil

On a lightly oiled cookie sheet, spread out the broccoli; sprinkle with lemon juice and then Parmesan cheese. Using an oil sprayer, spray a light coat of olive oil over the broccoli, and bake at 350° for 30–40 minutes or until the broccoli is cooked to your liking.

NUTRITIONAL DATA
Data does not include olive oil due to varying amounts.
Calories: 89
Total Fat: 2g
Saturated Fat: 1g
Trans Fat: 0g
Cholesterol: 4mg
Sodium: 131mg
Carbohydrates: 14g
Dietary Fiber: 5g
Sugars: 4g
Protein: 7g

Fava Beans with Garlic and Lemon

YIELD: 6 SERVINGS   SERVING SIZE: ¼ CUP

Fava beans are low in cholesterol and a good source of dietary fiber, folate, and vitamin K.

1 cup fava beans, shelled
1 tablespoon extra virgin olive oil
2 garlic cloves, minced
1 tablespoon chopped flat leaf parsley
1 tablespoon freshly squeezed lemon juice
½ teaspoon sea or kosher salt
Black pepper to taste

NUTRITIONAL DATA	
Calories: 80	Sodium: 227mg
Total Fat: 4g	Carbohydrates: 9g
Saturated Fat: 0g	Dietary Fiber: 2g
Trans Fat: 0g	Sugars: 1g
Cholesterol: 0mg	Protein: 3g

In a large pot, add fava beans, cover with water, bring to a boil, reduce heat to low, and simmer 3 minutes. Drain beans, return to pot, and add enough cold water to cover. After 5 minutes, drain, and remove and discard outer skins.

In a medium skillet, heat oil to medium low; add garlic, and sauté until fragrant, about 1 minute. Add beans and parsley, and continue sautéing another 5 minutes. Remove from heat, drizzle beans with lemon juice, salt, and pepper to taste.

Roasted Garlicky Cauliflower

YIELD: 4 SERVINGS   SERVING SIZE: ¼ RECIPE

1 medium head cauliflower, chopped bite-size
2 egg whites, beaten
1 teaspoon garlic powder
½ cup grated Parmesan cheese

NUTRITIONAL DATA
Calories: 100
Total Fat: 4g
Saturated Fat: 2g
Trans Fat: 0g
Cholesterol: 11mg
Sodium 262mg
Carbohydrates: 9g
Dietary Fiber: 4g
Sugars: 4g
Protein: 10g

Line a cookie sheet with parchment paper. In a food-safe plastic bag, combine the cauliflower, egg whites, garlic powder, and Parmesan cheese. Shake well to coat the cauliflower. Pour out onto the cookie sheet, and bake at 350° for 20–30 minutes or until the edges just begin to turn golden brown. Allow to cool, then serve.

Coconut Curry Cauliflower

YIELD: 3 SERVINGS   SERVING SIZE: ⅔ CUP

This side with its hints of Indian cuisine is sure to excite the pallet. Healthy is an understatement when it comes to this dish. A bowl of Coconut Curry Cauliflower is packed with nutrients: thiamin, riboflavin, niacin, folate, phosphorus, copper, calcium, iron, magnesium, potassium, and vitamins A, C, and K.

1 garlic clove, minced

2 teaspoons extra virgin olive oil

2 cups cauliflower florets

1 cup lite coconut milk, canned

1 teaspoon curry powder

½ teaspoon black pepper

¼ teaspoon crushed red pepper flakes

⅓ cup chopped fresh cilantro

Salt to taste

In a medium saucepan, sauté garlic in oil over medium-low heat until tender, about 4 minutes.

NUTRITIONAL DATA	
Calories: 190	Sodium: 99mg
Total Fat: 9g	Carbohydrates: 25g
Saturated Fat: 2g	Dietary Fiber: 6g
Trans Fat: 0g	Sugars: 3g
Cholesterol: 0mg	Protein: 10g

Combine remaining ingredients in the saucepan with garlic. Cover, and cook on medium-low heat until it begins to boil, then reduce heat, and simmer until cauliflower is tender, about 15 minutes.

Quinoa with Sun-Dried Tomato and Basil Pesto

Quinoa with Sun-Dried Tomato and Basil Pesto

YIELD: 18 SERVINGS   SERVING SIZE: 2 TABLESPOONS

Try this pesto on your favorite pasta or as a spread. Regardless, this is one delicious Italian treat. Quinoa may help in lessening the occurrence of migraine headaches with its levels of the nutrients vitamin B2 and magnesium.

1 cup white quinoa
2 cups low-sodium vegetable broth

Rinse quinoa, if not already pre-rinsed, using a colander. Be careful that colander does not have large drain holes, as the quinoa is very tiny and will be lost in the rinsing. In a medium saucepan, add quinoa to vegetable broth. Cover quinoa, bring to a boil, reduce heat to a simmer, and cook 15 minutes or until broth is absorbed. Prepare pesto while cooking.

SUN-DRIED TOMATO AND BASIL PESTO:

3 tablespoons pine nuts, lightly toasted
1 (8-ounce) jar sun-dried tomatoes, packed in olive oil, do not drain oil (we prefer Mezzetta brand)
1 tablespoon extra virgin olive oil
1 garlic clove
½ cup fresh basil leaves, packed
½ cup freshly grated Parmigiano-Reggiano cheese
Sea salt and black pepper to taste

Preheat oven to 350°.

Lightly toast pine nuts on a cookie sheet until fragrant, about 6 minutes. Allow to cool at room temperature.

Add all ingredients to a food processor, and pulse until puréed. Store in a glass jar with lid; refrigerate until ready to use. Add 2 tablespoons pesto to 2 cups cooked quinoa, more or less to taste.

NUTRITIONAL DATA
Calories: 60
Total Fat: 4g
Saturated Fat: 1g
Trans Fat: 0g
Cholesterol: 1mg
Sodium: 31mg
Carbohydrates: 6g
Dietary Fiber: 1g
Sugars: 3g
Protein: 2g

Refried Beans

YIELD: 4 SERVINGS   SERVING SIZE: 1 CUP

Beans, such as pintos, are often referred to as "poor man's meat" because of their high protein content and low cost. Beans are an excellent source of phytochemicals, which have disease-fighting antioxidants. Dried beans may also help to lower the risk of estrogen-related cancers . . . good news on the fight against breast cancer.

1 tablespoon extra virgin olive oil

1 tablespoon diced onion

1 garlic clove, minced

2 (15-ounce) cans pinto beans, drained

½ cup low-sodium vegetable broth

¼ teaspoon cumin

¼ teaspoon black pepper

Salt to taste

1 tablespoon chopped fresh cilantro

Shredded cheese and plain, nonfat Greek-style yogurt for garnish

NUTRITIONAL DATA	
Calories: 338	Sodium: 24mg
Total Fat: 5g	Carbohydrates: 57g
Saturated Fat: 1g	Dietary Fiber: 19g
Trans Fat: 0g	Sugars: 1g
Cholesterol: 0mg	Protein: 19g

In a large skillet, add oil; heat over medium-low heat. Add onion and garlic; sauté until tender, approximately 4 minutes. Combine remaining ingredients in a large mixing bowl. Using a potato masher, mash bean mixture until desired consistency.

Add mashed bean mixture to skillet with onion and garlic, and heat until warm. Remove from heat, and top with shredded cheese and Greek-style yogurt, if desired.

Mexican Rice

YIELD: 4 SERVINGS   SERVING SIZE: 1 CUP

This side pairs well with Steak Fajita Sandwiches (page 141) and Spinach Enchilada Solo (page 172). This yummy dish has zero grams of saturated fat and cholesterol, and it's an excellent source of dietary fiber, thiamin, calcium, magnesium, potassium, copper, iron, and vitamins A, C and K. Brown rice is a natural detoxifier that assists in removing toxins in the body.

1 garlic clove, minced

½ cup diced onion

1 tablespoon extra virgin olive oil

1 cup long-grain brown rice

1 teaspoon cumin

Salt to taste

½ teaspoon black pepper

½ cup diced carrots

½ cup frozen peas

⅓ cup chopped fresh cilantro

1 (10-ounce) can diced tomatoes with green chiles

2 cups fat-free, low-sodium chicken broth

NUTRITIONAL DATA

Calories: 139	Sodium: 371mg
Total Fat: 0g	Carbohydrates: 23g
Saturated Fat: 0g	Dietary Fiber: 4g
Trans Fat: 0g	Sugars: 4g
Cholesterol: 0mg	Protein: 7g

In a large skillet or saucepan, sauté garlic and onion in oil over medium-low heat until tender, about 4 minutes. Add rice, cumin, salt, and pepper, and continue cooking for 3 minutes. Add remaining ingredients, cover, reduce heat, and simmer on low for 30 minutes, or until rice has soaked up most of the liquid and is tender.

Cajun-Style Rice Blend

Wild and brown rice are excellent sources of vitamins C and K, and are low in saturated fat and cholesterol. Spice up the dinner with a side that's easy to prepare and sure to please.

YIELD: 4 SERVINGS   SERVING SIZE: 1 CUP

1 tablespoon extra virgin olive oil

½ cup diced yellow onion

1 garlic clove, minced

½ cup diced green bell pepper

1 celery stalk, diced

½ cup diced tomatoes

1 teaspoon dried oregano

½ teaspoon dried basil

½ teaspoon paprika

½ teaspoon black pepper

¼ teaspoon chili powder

¼ teaspoon cayenne pepper

¼ teaspoon crushed red pepper flakes

Salt to taste

2 tablespoons tomato paste

1 cup wild and brown rice blend (we like Lundberg Wild Blend)

2 cups fat-free low-sodium chicken broth

NUTRITIONAL DATA

Calories: 205	Sodium: 89mg
Total Fat: 4g	Carbohydrates: 37g
Saturated Fat: 1g	Dietary Fiber: 4g
Trans Fat: 0g	Sugars: 3g
Cholesterol: 0mg	Protein: 6g

In a large pot, add oil; turn to medium-low heat. Add onion, garlic, bell pepper, celery, and tomatoes; sauté until tender, about 5 minutes. Add spices, tomato paste, rice, and broth; stir. Bring to a boil, cover with lid, reduce heat, and simmer 50 minutes, or until rice is al dente. Stir every 15 minutes to prevent sticking. Leave pot covered 5–10 minutes before serving.

Sandwiches, Pizzas, and Quesadillas

Caramelized Onion Sliders with Mushrooms and BBQ Chicken

Caramelized Onion Sliders with Mushrooms and BBQ Chicken

YIELD: 8 SERVINGS   SERVING SIZE: 1 SLIDER

These little sandwiches are full on flavor while being an excellent source of niacin. The Creamy Cabbage and Bok Choy Slaw adds a nice touch while lending support to a strong immune system.

3 chicken breast fillets (1 pound)

2 tablespoons olive oil, divided

½ cup barbecue sauce, no sugar added

½ teaspoon black pepper

1 large sweet onion, sliced into thin rings

4 ounces white mushrooms, sliced

8 small whole-wheat buns or rolls

2 tablespoons Creamy Cabbage and Bok Choy Slaw (page 98)

Salt to taste

> NUTRITIONAL DATA
> Calories: 297
> Total Fat: 8g
> Saturated Fat: 2g
> Trans Fat: 0g
> Cholesterol: 49mg
> Sodium: 265mg
> Carbohydrates: 32g
> Dietary Fiber: 4g
> Sugars: 7g
> Protein: 24g

Cut chicken fillets into ½-inch thick slices; cook in 1 tablespoon olive oil on medium-high heat until it loses its pink color and begins to brown, about 10 minutes. Add barbecue sauce, reduce heat to medium, and continue cooking uncovered until chicken has soaked up most of the sauce. In the meantime, prepare onion and mushrooms.

In a medium skillet, add remaining 1 tablespoon oil; turn heat to low. When oil is hot but not smoking, add onion, and cook until caramelized, approximately 15 minutes. Add mushrooms, and continue cooking until mushrooms release moisture and are tender, approximately 6 more minutes.

Place slightly warmed buns or rolls on a prep space; evenly distribute chicken slices. Next, top chicken with onion and mushrooms. Top off sliders with Creamy Cabbage and Bok Choy Cole Slaw. Add salt to taste.

Chicken Sandwiches with Sun-Dried Tomatoes, Avocado, and Mozzarella

YIELD: 4 SERVINGS   SERVING SIZE: 1 SANDWICH

Chicken pairs perfectly with the superfoods layered on this ultra juicy sandwich.

2 teaspoons canola oil

4 (4-ounce) skinless chicken fillets, thinly sliced

Sea salt and black pepper to taste

4 pieces artisan whole-grain bread, sliced horizontally

¼ cup shredded low-fat mozzarella cheese, divided

12 sun-dried tomato slices, packed in olive oil

1 avocado, peeled, thinly sliced

¼ cup Basil-Garlic Sauce (page 138)

NUTRITIONAL DATA	
Calories: 381	Sodium: 494mg
Total Fat: 14g	Carbohydrates: 27g
Saturated Fat: 4g	Dietary Fiber: 6g
Trans Fat: 0g	Sugars: 5g
Cholesterol: 81mg	Protein: 36g

Preheat oven to 375°. Add oil to skillet, turn to medium heat, and add chicken fillets. Season with salt and pepper to taste. Cook chicken until crispy on both sides, and juices run clear when pierced with a fork.

Prepare toast while chicken is cooking. Add cut sides of whole-grain bread to a cookie sheet; lightly toast. Add 1 tablespoon mozzarella and sun-dried tomatoes to 4 slices of bread; continue toasting until cheese melts and tomatoes are soft. Remove from oven, and top with cooked chicken and avocado. Spread Basil-Garlic Sauce on bread slices without toppings. Sandwich bread pieces together.

Tomato and Roasted Pepper Panini

YIELD: 4 SERVINGS   SERVING SIZE: 1 PANINI

Want better vision and stronger immunity? Have one of these small Italian sandwiches, and you're on the right track. Also, this sandwich is low in cholesterol and a good source of vitamins A and C.

1 bell pepper, seeded

1½ tablespoons extra virgin olive oil, divided

6 slices whole-grain artisan bread

4 slices sweet onion

4 slices tomato

4 tablespoons spreadable goat cheese

1 tablespoon chopped fresh thyme or basil

Salt and pepper to taste

Preheat oven to 400°.

Slice bell pepper into fourths, and place on a cookie sheet; drizzle with 2 teaspoons olive oil; roast 20 minutes. Cool slightly before removing peeling.

NUTRITIONAL DATA

Calories: 306	Sodium: 296mg
Total Fat: 16g	Carbohydrates: 31g
Saturated Fat: 5g	Dietary Fiber: 6g
Trans Fat: 0g	Sugars: 8g
Cholesterol: 11mg	Protein: 11g

Brush side of each bread slice with remaining oil. Heat either panini press or nonstick skillet to 350° or medium heat. Evenly distribute remaining ingredients to 3 slices of bread. Place other slice of bread on top, oil side up.

Heat panini until bread is crispy and all are ingredients hot.

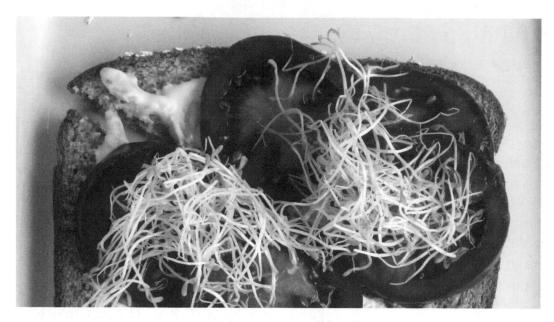

Open-Faced Sandwiches with Kumatoes, Sprouts, and Yogurt Spread

YIELD: 4 SERVINGS   SERVING SIZE: 1 SANDWICH

If you can find Kumato-style tomatoes in your area, you have to give these little jewels a try. They have a mild flavor and incredible taste. These brightly colored tomatoes are associated with lowering the risk of breast and prostate cancer, as well as being a good source of potassium and selenium.

½ cup plain, nonfat Greek-style yogurt

1 teaspoon extra virgin olive oil

1 teaspoon freshly squeezed lemon juice

1 teaspoon mild-flavored honey, light in color

⅛ teaspoon freshly ground black pepper

2 tablespoons raw pine nuts

4 slices 12-grain bread

4 Kumato-style tomatoes, sliced (or your favorite tomato)

1 cup broccoli sprouts

NUTRITIONAL DATA	
Calories: 226	Sodium: 213mg
Total Fat: 8g	Carbohydrates: 29g
Saturated Fat: 1g	Dietary Fiber: 3g
Trans Fat: 0g	Sugars: 6g
Cholesterol: 1mg	Protein: 5g

In a small mixing bowl, add the first 6 ingredients; stir to combine. Lightly toast bread, add 1 tablespoon yogurt spread to each half, and top with sliced tomatoes and ¼ cup broccoli sprouts. Garnish with additional pine nuts, if desired.

Quinoa-Lentil Veggie Patties

YIELD: 4 SERVINGS   SERVING SIZE: 1 BURGER

2 tablespoons canola oil, divided
¼ cup diced red onion
1 carrot, peeled and finely diced
1 cup cooked green lentils, drained
1 cup white quinoa
1 cup rolled oats
½ teaspoon cumin
¼ teaspoon garlic powder
⅓ cup panko whole-wheat bread crumbs or white whole-wheat flour

In a large skillet, add 1 tablespoon canola oil, turn to medium-low heat, and sauté onion and diced carrot until tender, 6–8 minutes. In a large mixing bowl, mash together lentils and quinoa, using a potato masher or fork. Add sautéed onion, carrot, and remaining ingredients; stir to combine.

NUTRITIONAL DATA

Calories: 430	Sodium: 34mg
Total Fat: 9g	Carbohydrates: 73g
Saturated Fat: 1g	Dietary Fiber: 13g
Trans Fat: 0g	Sugars: 4g
Cholesterol: 0mg	Protein: 17g

Make 4 burger-shaped patties. Or, using a large circular cookie cutter, pack and press mixture to form patties. Add remaining tablespoon of canola oil to a large skillet, turn to medium heat, and cook until patties are browned on both sides, approximately 6 minutes on each side.

Serve patties on your favorite whole-grain bun or roll.

Vegetarian Veggie Sandwiches

Vegetarian Veggie Sandwiches

YIELD: 4 SERVINGS   SERVING SIZE: 1 SANDWICH

4¼ slices red bell peppers, cored, seeded, roasted

1 tablespoon plus 2 teaspoons extra virgin olive oil, divided

8 ounces white mushrooms, sliced

4 pieces artisan whole-grain bread, sliced horizontally

¼ cup low-fat shredded mozzarella cheese

1 avocado, peeled and thinly sliced

2 Roma tomatoes, thinly sliced

1 cup arugula

¼ cup Basil-Garlic Sauce

NUTRITIONAL DATA

Calories: 258	Sodium: 310mg
Total Fat: 12g	Carbohydrates: 31g
Saturated Fat: 3g	Dietary Fiber: 7g
Trans Fat: 0g	Sugars: 7g
Cholesterol: 7mg	Protein: 11g

Preheat oven to 375°.

Slice bell peppers into fourths, place on a cookie sheet, drizzle with 2 teaspoons extra virgin olive oil, and roast for 20 minutes. Allow to cool slightly before removing skin. (Roasted peppers can be purchased at your local grocery.)

In a small skillet, add 1 tablespoon oil, heat to medium low, and sauté mushrooms until soft, about 6 minutes.

While mushrooms sauté, place bread, cut sides up, on a cookie sheet; lightly toast. On half the slices, add 1 tablespoon mozzarella to each; continue toasting until cheese melts. Remove from oven, and top cheese slices with mushrooms and bell peppers. Evenly distribute avocado slices, Roma tomatoes, and arugula on top of peppers.

Spread Basil-Garlic Sauce on remaining plain bread slices, and top filled slices.

BASIL-GARLIC SAUCE:

YIELD: 4 SERVINGS   SERVING SIZE: 1 TABLESPOON

½ cup packed fresh basil

3 garlic cloves

¼ cup pine nuts

¼ cup grated Parmigiano-Reggiano cheese

Sea salt to taste

¼ cup extra virgin olive oil

NUTRITIONAL DATA

Calories: 157	Sodium: 77mg
Total Fat: 16g	Carbohydrates: 2g
Saturated Fat: 2g	Dietary Fiber: 0g
Trans Fat: 0g	Sugars: 0g
Cholesterol: 4mg	Protein: 2g

Add all ingredients to a food processor, and pulse until combined and smooth. Pour into a glass container with lid; store in the refrigerator until ready to use.

Salmon Patties with Lentils

YIELD: 4 SERVINGS   SERVING SIZE: 1 PATTY

Salmon is filled with omega-3 fatty acids. The omega-3's can help in lowering cholesterol, and possibly relieve symptoms of rheumatoid arthritis.

1 (8-ounce) wild Alaskan salmon fillet, or 1 (14-ounce) can salmon, drained

1 tablespoon extra virgin olive oil

1 large egg, slightly beaten

½ cup cooked lentils, drained

¼ cup finely diced red onion

¼ cup roasted and diced red bell pepper

½ cup whole-wheat panko or whole-wheat bread crumbs

⅛ teaspoon cayenne

½ teaspoon black pepper

¼ teaspoon thyme

Sea salt to taste

1 tablespoon canola oil

NUTRITIONAL DATA	
Calories: 312	Sodium: 101mg
Total Fat: 14g	Carbohydrates: 26g
Saturated Fat: 2g	Dietary Fiber: 5g
Trans Fat: 0g	Sugars: 2g
Cholesterol: 93mg	Protein: 22g

Preheat oven to broil.

Line a rimmed cookie sheet with foil; spread olive oil on both sides of salmon, and place on cookie sheet, skin side down. Broil on both sides 5–6 minutes, or until it reaches an internal temperature of 131°. Allow to cool, then remove skin.

Place salmon in a medium mixing bowl, and flake, using a fork. Add egg, lentils, onion, bell pepper, panko, and spices to salmon; mash either by hand or using a potato masher. Shape salmon into 4 patties. Or, using a large circular cookie cutter, pack and press salmon mixture to form patties.

Add canola oil to a large skillet, turn to medium heat, and cook patties on each side for about 5 minutes or until cooked through and lightly browned.

Serve salmon patties as a main dish or as a burger-style sandwich with your favorite condiments.

Steak Fajita Sandwiches

YIELD: 4 SERVINGS   SERVING SIZE: ½ PITA POCKET WITH ¼ MEAT FILLING

This easy-to-make sandwich goes great with a serving of Mexican Rice (page 129) and Refried Beans (page 128). Eat this fajita sandwich and you'll not only get plenty of protein, but add to that a wealth of niacin, phosphorus, zinc, selenium, and vitamins B6 and B12.

NUTRITIONAL DATA

Calories: 255	Sodium: 235mg
Total Fat: 6g	Carbohydrates: 21g
Saturated Fat: 2g	Dietary Fiber: 3g
Trans Fat: 0g	Sugars: 2g
Cholesterol: 70mg	Protein: 29g

4 ounces white mushrooms, sliced

1 tablespoon olive oil

1 medium red onion, sliced into strips

2 garlic cloves, minced

1 medium red bell pepper, cut into strips

1 pound beef sirloin tip steak, cut into thin strips (grass-fed beef recommended)

Salt to taste

½ teaspoon black pepper

2 teaspoons dried oregano

2 whole-wheat pita pockets, cut in half

4 leaves romaine lettuce, torn

¼ cup plain, nonfat Greek-style yogurt

In a large skillet, on medium-low heat, sauté mushrooms in olive oil about 6 minutes. Add onion, garlic, and bell pepper, and continue sautéing until onion and pepper are tender, about 4 minutes. Add in sirloin strips, and cook on medium heat for 5–10 minutes, or until no longer pink. Sprinkle with salt, pepper, and oregano. Stir well, cover, and simmer 5 more minutes. Drain mixture.

Stuff pita halves with meat mixture and romaine lettuce, and top with a dollop of yogurt.

Chicken Gyro with Baby Spinach

YIELD: 4 SERVINGS   SERVING SIZE: ½ PITA POCKET, STUFFED

The yogurt sauce used in this sandwich contains lactic acid, which makes calcium easier to digest and more beneficial toward the prevention of bone loss. This sandwich overall is a good source of vitamins A and K, niacin, and protein.

1 tablespoon extra virgin olive oil

1 small mildly flavored onion, diced

2 boneless, skinless chicken breasts, thinly sliced

½ teaspoon black pepper

2 teaspoons dried oregano

½ teaspoon onion flakes

½ teaspoon garlic powder

Salt to taste

Pinch of nutmeg

1 cup baby spinach

2 pita pockets, cut in half

12 cherry or grape tomatoes

Mediterranean Tzatziki Yogurt Sauce (page 33)

Preheat oven to 350°.

In a medium skillet, add oil; turn to medium-low heat, and sauté onion until tender, about 4 minutes. Add chicken, raise heat to medium-high, and continue cooking until it loses it pink color. Sprinkle chicken with black pepper, oregano, onion flakes, garlic powder, salt, and nutmeg. Cover chicken, and continue cooking until brown, approximately 10 minutes.

Warm pita pockets for 2–3 minutes. Stuff slightly warmed pita pockets with chicken, spinach, tomatoes, and Mediterranean Tzatziki Yogurt Sauce.

NUTRITIONAL DATA	
Calories: 230	Sodium: 250mg
Total Fat: 9g	Carbohydrates: 19g
Saturated Fat: 2g	Dietary Fiber: 4g
Trans Fat: 0g	Sugars: 5g
Cholesterol: 46mg	Protein: 20g

Tip: Try these fillings in your gyro: lamb, romaine lettuce, bell peppers, mushrooms, feta cheese, or eggplant.

Spinach and Mushroom Quesadilla

YIELD: 1 SERVING   SERVING SIZE: ENTIRE RECIPE

1 large garlic clove, chopped
¼ pound cremini mushrooms, sliced (brown
mushrooms)
1 cup raw spinach, tightly packed
1 teaspoon olive oil
¼ cup freshly grated mozzarella
1 large whole-wheat tortilla

Preheat oven to 350°.

In a large frying pan, sauté the garlic, mushrooms, and spinach in the olive oil over low to medium heat.

Place tortilla on a parchment-lined cookie sheet. Sprinkle the cheese over half of the tortilla. When the vegetables are done, spread them over the cheese and fold the tortilla in half.

Bake for 10–15 minutes, or until the cheese is melted and the tortilla just starts to turn golden brown around the edges.

Allow to cool slightly, cut in half, and enjoy.

Note: Whole-wheat tortillas vary greatly in nutritional data. For this reason, the nutritional data is for the filling only. Please add the data for the tortilla you use to this data.

NUTRITIONAL DATA
Data does not include tortilla.
Calories: 233
Total Fat: 14g
Saturated Fat: 6g
Trans Fat: 0g
Cholesterol: 36mg
Sodium: 379mg
Carbohydrates: 10g
Dietary Fiber: 2g
Sugars: 3g
Protein: 18g

Red Pepper and Spinach Quesadilla

Red Pepper and Spinach Quesadilla

YIELD: 1 SERVING   SERVING SIZE: ENTIRE RECIPE

This quesadilla is a full meal unto itself. It will fill you up and satisfy your cravings for a flavorful meal. It's also a great way to get vitamins A, C, and K.

1 cup raw spinach, tightly packed

2 garlic cloves, finely chopped

½ cup finely chopped red onion

1 teaspoon olive oil

1 large whole-wheat tortilla

½ cup finely chopped red bell pepper

¼ cup finely grated Jack cheese

Salt to taste (optional)

Over low heat, sauté the spinach, garlic, and onion in the olive oil 2–3 minutes or until the spinach is wilted. Spread this over a whole-wheat tortilla, top with the bell pepper, cheese, and salt, if desired, and bake at 350° for 10–15 minutes or until the cheese is completely melted. Fold in half, allow to cool, and serve.

NUTRITIONAL DATA
Data does not include tortilla.

Calories: 243	Sodium: 212mg
Total Fat: 14g	Carbohydrates: 21g
Saturated Fat: 6g	Dietary Fiber: 4g
Trans Fat: 0g	Sugars: 12g
Cholesterol: 27mg	Protein: 10g

Note: Whole-wheat tortillas vary greatly in nutritional data. For this reason, the nutritional data is for the filling only. Please add the data for the tortilla you use to this data.

Mango and Cilantro Quesadilla

YIELD: 1 SERVING   SERVING SIZE: ENTIRE RECIPE

This is a filling meal with lots of calcium, and vitamins A and C. It's a bit higher in fat, so balance this out with your meal plan for the remainder of the day. All things can be enjoyed in balance and moderation.

1 large whole-wheat tortilla
½ cup finely chopped fresh mango
1 tablespoon chopped fresh cilantro
¼ cup finely grated Jack cheese

On the large, whole-wheat tortilla, layer the mango and cilantro, and top with cheese. Bake at 350° for 10–15 minutes, or until the cheese is completely melted. Cool slightly, fold in half, and cut into triangles.

> **NUTRITIONAL DATA**
> Data does not include tortilla.
>
> Calories: 165   Sodium: 173mg
> Total Fat: 9g   Carbohydrates: 15g
> Saturated Fat: 6g   Dietary Fiber: 2g
> Trans Fat: 0g   Sugars: 12g
> Cholesterol: 27mg   Protein: 7g

Note: Whole-wheat tortillas vary greatly in nutritional data. For this reason, the nutritional data is for the filling only. Please add the data for the tortilla you use to this data.

Pizza Quesadilla

YIELD: 1 SERVING   SERVING SIZE: 1 QUESADILLA

This is the easiest way to make pizza at the last minute . . . and tasty, too!

¼ cup Easy Pizza Sauce (below)
1 large whole-wheat tortilla
½ cup finely chopped red onion
¼ cup raw spinach, tightly packed
¼ cup finely chopped mushrooms
¼ cup chopped black olives
  (optional)
¼ cup finely grated Jack cheese

Spread the sauce over the large, whole-wheat tortilla. Layer vegetables, and top with cheese. Bake at 350° for 10–15 minutes, or until the cheese is melted. Allow to cool. Fold in half, slice, and serve.

NUTRITIONAL DATA
Data does not include tortilla or optional ingredients.

Calories: 197	Sodium: 541mg
Total Fat: 9g	Carbohydrates: 21g
Saturated Fat: 6g	Dietary Fiber: 3g
Trans Fat: 0g	Sugars: 10g
Cholesterol: 27mg	Protein: 10g

Note: Whole-wheat tortillas vary greatly in nutritional data. For this reason, the nutritional data is for the filling only. Please add the data for the tortilla you use to this data.

Easy Pizza Sauce

YIELD: 3 SERVINGS   SERVING SIZE: ½ CUP

This simple sauce will leave you wondering why you ever used store-bought sauce!

1 (15-ounce) can tomato sauce, no
  sugar added
1 teaspoon garlic powder
1 teaspoon onion powder
2 teaspoons dry basil
½ teaspoon dry oregano

Whisk all ingredients together in a mixing bowl, and use as desired.

Note: Choose low-sodium tomato sauce to lower sodium content.

NUTRITIONAL DATA
Sodium content will vary based on tomato sauce used.

Calories: 53	Sodium: 701mg
Total Fat: 0g	Carbohydrates: 13g
Saturated Fat: 0g	Dietary Fiber: 3g
Trans Fat: 0g	Sugars: 3g
Cholesterol: 0mg	Protein: 3g

Italian Herb Pizza Dough

YIELD: 1 SERVING   SERVING SIZE: 15 PIECES

This recipe puts a flavorful spin on a classic whole-grain pizza dough by adding herbs to the dough itself. The dough is soft and bready with just the perfect amount of flavor that will enhance any toppings you add to it.

1 tablespoon honey
2 cups warm water (105°–115°)
1 packet active dry yeast
4 cups white whole-wheat flour
1 teaspoon sea salt
2 tablespoons Italian seasoning (herb blend)
2 tablespoons olive oil plus extra for coating

In a medium cup, dissolve honey in warm water, and gently stir in yeast. Allow to sit for at least 10–15 minutes, or until the top becomes completely foamy.

In a large mixing bowl, whisk together flour, salt, and Italian seasoning.

Pour the yeast mixture into the flour, followed by the oil, and stir with a wooden spoon until it becomes too difficult to stir. Then continue kneading with your hands for approximately 5 minutes. The dough should be slightly sticky.

Form dough into a nice round ball, and set in the middle of your mixing bowl. Using your hands, coat the dough in a light layer of olive oil to keep it from drying out. Cover bowl with a dish towel, and set in a warm place for 1 hour to rise. When dough is finished rising, beat it down with your fists, and roll it out into the size and shape you need for your pizza. There is no need to bake the crust prior to adding your toppings.

NUTRITIONAL DATA
Calories: 134
Total Fat: 2g
Saturated Fat: 0g
Trans Fat: 0g
Cholesterol: 0mg
Sodium: 158mg
Carbohydrates: 25g
Dietary Fiber: 4g
Sugars: 1g
Protein: 5g

Note: Data based on a pizza cooked on a full-size cookie sheet, and cut into 15 pieces.

Almond Mango Pita Pizza

YIELD: 1 SERVING   SERVING SIZE: ENTIRE RECIPE

Nuts are full of healthy fats. Eaten in moderation, they are a wonderfully tasty way to get your healthy fats for the day. And with this recipe, you can also enjoy a nice portion of vitamins C, A, and E.

2 tablespoons plain, nonfat Greek-style yogurt

1 teaspoon honey

1 whole-wheat pita, no sugar added

½ mango, peeled and chopped

¼ cup chopped almonds

Mix honey and yogurt together in a small mixing bowl. Spread over pita, and top with mango and almonds.

NUTRITIONAL DATA
Data does not include pita, which can vary greatly depending on brand used.

Calories: 259   Sodium: 11mg
Total Fat: 14g   Carbohydrates: 30g
Saturated Fat: 1g   Dietary Fiber: 5g
Trans Fat: 0g   Sugars: 23g
Cholesterol: 0mg   Protein: 9g

Artichoke and Sun-Dried Tomato Thin-Crust Pizza

Artichoke and Sun-Dried Tomato Thin-Crust Pizza

YIELD: 8 SERVINGS   SERVING SIZE: 1 SLICE

Until several years ago I had never tried artichokes. I was missing out on a food that has a wonderful mild taste, is versatile, and has many health benefits. This superfood is low in cholesterol and is a good source of dietary fiber, iron, potassium, copper, calcium, and vitamins A and C.

1 tablespoon olive oil
4 ounces white mushrooms, sliced
2 large garlic cloves, minced
8 ounces artichoke hearts, coarsely chopped
½ cup sun-dried tomatoes
½ cup pizza sauce, no added sweeteners
2 tablespoons chopped, stemmed fresh thyme
¼ cup grated Parmesan cheese
1 (10-inch) whole-wheat thin crust (Boboli Italian Thin Crust was used in this recipe)

NUTRITIONAL DATA
Calories: 198
Total Fat: 0g
Saturated Fat: 2g
Trans Fat: 0g
Cholesterol: 4mg
Sodium: 582mg
Carbohydrates: 30g
Dietary Fiber: 6g
Sugars: 5g
Protein: 9g

Preheat oven to 450°.

In a large skillet, add oil and sauté mushrooms on medium heat until tender, approximately 5 minutes. Add garlic, artichoke hearts, and sun-dried tomatoes, and continue cooking 1–2 minutes.

Spread sauce over the crust, leaving 1 inch around the edges dry. Evenly distribute onto crust, the mushroom mixture, thyme, and Parmesan cheese. Preferably place pizza directly onto middle oven rack. Otherwise, place pizza on a large cooking stone or cookie sheet. Bake 8–10 minutes.

Spinach and Pineapple Pizza on Curry Crust

YIELD: 15 SERVINGS   SERVING SIZE: 1 SLICE

This new twist on pizza will have your family coming back for more. And with all these healthy ingredients, you won't mind giving it to them!

DOUGH:

Follow the recipe for Italian Herb Pizza Dough (page 148), but substitute 1 tablespoon onion powder and 1 tablespoon curry powder for the Italian herb seasoning.

SAUCE:

1½ cups tomato sauce, no sugar added, or 1 (15-ounce) can

1 teaspoon curry powder

½ teaspoon cinnamon

TOPPINGS:

2 cups raw spinach

2 cups pineapple chunks (if canned, no sugar added)

1 large red onion, chopped

½ pound sliced mushrooms

1 cup finely shredded Jack cheese

NUTRITIONAL DATA	
Calories: 205	Sodium: 357mg
Total Fat: 5g	Carbohydrates: 34g
Saturated Fat: 2g	Dietary Fiber: 6g
Trans Fat: 0g	Sugars: 7g
Cholesterol: 8mg	Protein: 8g

Spread Dough out over a lightly oiled, full-size cookie sheet. Spread Sauce over Dough and layer the rest of the ingredients over that, with cheese being the top layer. Bake at 350° for 20–30 minutes or until the cheese is melted and pizza dough is completely cooked. Allow to cool, and serve.

Note: The sodium content can be reduced by using low- or no-sodium tomato sauce for the pizza sauce.

Skillet Mushroom Zucchini Pizza

YIELD: 15 SERVINGS   SERVING SIZE: 1 SLICE

You just can't beat a pizza that is not only delicious, but only 166 calories per slice! This fabulous dish will give you a nice serving of fiber, vitamin K, calcium, and iron.

1 batch Italian Herb Pizza Dough (page 148)
1 batch Easy Pizza Sauce (page 147)
1 large zucchini, grated
½ pound cremini mushrooms, sliced
½ cup sliced Parmesan cheese

NUTRITIONAL DATA

Calories: 166	Sodium: 352mg
Total Fat: 3g	Carbohydrates: 29g
Saturated Fat: 1g	Dietary Fiber: 5g
Trans Fat: 0g	Sugars: 3g
Cholesterol: 3mg	Protein: 7g

Make your dough, and break off a piece just large enough to cover the bottom of your skillet (any size). It should come up on the side of the pan just slightly to help keep the sauce and toppings from leaking off during baking. Spread on the sauce, and then add the zucchini and mushrooms. Top off with Parmesan cheese, and bake for about 20 minutes at 350° on the bottom shelf of your oven. During the last 5 minutes of baking, turn your oven to broil, and set the pan on the top shelf to brown everything nicely (if necessary).

Zucchini-Bell Pepper Pizza

YIELD: 8 SERVINGS   SERVING SIZE: 1 SLICE

Here's proof that healthy tastes great while helping to give our bodies the necessary nutrients to fight disease. This colorful pizza packs a hefty amount of vitamin C, vitamin B, potassium, and phytochemicals, which may help in providing protection against cancer.

1 tablespoon extra virgin olive oil

2 garlic cloves, minced

1 small red onion, cut in half then thinly sliced

1 cup sliced bell peppers (try the recipe for Balsamic Bell Peppers on page 121)

1 small zucchini, sliced

½ cup pizza sauce, no added sweeteners

1 (10- or 12-inch) whole-wheat thin pizza crust (Boboli Italian Thin Crust was used in this recipe)

½ cup diced sun-dried tomatoes, or 2 Roma tomatoes, sliced

8 green olives, diced

1 tablespoon chopped fresh basil

½ cup shredded 2% mozzarella cheese

NUTRITIONAL DATA	
Calories: 115	Sodium: 280mg
Total Fat: 7g	Carbohydrates: 10g
Saturated Fat: 2g	Dietary Fiber: 2g
Trans Fat: 0g	Sugars: 3g
Cholesterol: 8mg	Protein: 6g

Preheat oven to 450°.

In a large skillet, add oil, and sauté on medium-low heat for 1 minute, the garlic, onion, bell peppers (if using the Balsamic Bell Pepper recipe, do not sauté with the other ingredients), and zucchini slices.

Spread sauce over the crust, leaving 1 inch around the edges dry. Evenly distribute onto crust the garlic, onion, bell peppers, zucchini, sun-dried to-matoes, olives, basil, and mozzarella cheese. Preferably, place pizza directly onto middle oven rack. Otherwise, place pizza on a large cooking stone or cookie sheet. Bake 10 minutes or until cheese is melted.

Main Dishes

Chicken Drumsticks over Quinoa

Chicken Drumsticks over Quinoa

YIELD: 6 SERVINGS   SERVING SIZE: 1 DRUMSTICK AND 1 CUP QUINOA

1 tablespoon olive oil

6 chicken drumsticks, skins removed (free-range is best)

1 garlic clove, minced

1 large shallot, diced

1 (14½-ounce) can petit diced tomatoes in all natural juice

1 tablespoon chopped fresh oregano, or 2 teaspoons dried oregano

1 tablespoon capers, drained

½ teaspoon crushed red pepper flakes

Salt to taste

½ teaspoon freshly ground pepper

½ cup fat-free, low-sodium chicken broth

2 cups cooked white quinoa, cooked according to package directions

NUTRITIONAL DATA
Calories: 294
Total Fat: 10g
Saturated Fat: 2g
Trans Fat: 0g
Cholesterol: 90mg
Sodium: 145mg
Carbohydrates: 19g
Dietary Fiber: 3g
Sugars: 2g
Protein: 30g

In a large skillet, add oil, and turn to medium heat; add chicken, and brown on both sides, about 15 minutes. Remove chicken, and place on a plate lined with a paper towel. Add garlic and shallot to skillet, reduce heat to medium-low, and sauté until tender, about 4 minutes. Add tomatoes, oregano, capers, red pepper flakes, salt, pepper, and broth. Cover, turn heat to low, and cook until chicken is done, about 30 minutes. Add cooked quinoa to skillet, toss, and cook another 2 minutes. Place quinoa and tomatoes on a serving platter with chicken on top.

Cabbage with Apples and Chicken

YIELD: 8 CUPS   SERVING SIZE: 1 CUP

Get plenty of vitamins C and K and niacin in this wonderfully flavorful dish. The different textures and flavors blend together beautifully for a very appetizing and nutritious dish.

2 boneless skinless chicken breasts (about 7 ounces each)

Juice of 1 lemon

½ medium head red cabbage, quartered and sliced

1 cup finely chopped red onion

1 tablespoon balsamic vinegar

1½ cups chopped apples

1 tablespoon caraway seeds

3 garlic cloves, chopped

Juice of 1 lemon

1 tablespoon honey

½ cup low-sodium chicken broth, no sugar added

NUTRITIONAL DATA	
Calories: 124	Sodium: 58mg
Total Fat: 2g	Carbohydrates: 14g
Saturated Fat: 0g	Dietary Fiber: 2g
Trans Fat: 0g	Sugars: 9g
Cholesterol: 24mg	Protein: 13g

Place the chicken on a parchment-lined cookie sheet, and sprinkle the lemon juice over it. Bake at 350° about 45 minutes or until done (at least 165° internal temperature).

In a large skillet, combine remaining ingredients, and cook until cabbage is wilted. When the chicken is done baking, cut into bite-sized pieces, and stir it into the cabbage mixture. Allow to cool slightly, and serve.

Curry Pineapple Chicken Rice Bowl

YIELD: 10 SERVINGS   SERVING SIZE: 1 CUP

A wonderful source of protein, manganese, and niacin, this filling dish is the perfect way to get your family around the table.

6 boneless skinless chicken breasts (about 7 ounces each)

1 tablespoon curry powder

1 teaspoon ground cinnamon

½ teaspoon ground ginger

1½ cups dry brown rice

1 (20-ounce) can pineapple and juice, no sugar added

2¾ cups low-sodium chicken broth

1 cup shredded raw carrots

1 cup shredded raw zucchini

Salt to taste (optional)

NUTRITIONAL DATA
Calories: 297
Total Fat: 6g
Saturated Fat: 1g
Trans Fat: 0g
Cholesterol: 57mg
Sodium: 104mg
Carbohydrates: 29g
Dietary Fiber: 2g
Sugars: 5g
Protein: 30g

Place chicken breasts on a parchment-lined cookie sheet, and sprinkle spices over the top. Bake at 350° for approximately 45 minutes, or until internal temperature of the meat reaches at least 165°. Remove from oven, cool, and cut into bite-sized pieces.

While chicken is baking, cook rice in pineapple juice and chicken broth. When fully cooked, remove from heat, and stir in carrots, zucchini, pineapple, and chicken, and serve. Season with salt, if desired.

Lemon Basil and Almond Chicken

YIELD: 8 SERVINGS   SERVING SIZE: 1 CUP

4 boneless skinless chicken breasts (about 7 ounces each)

Juice of 2 lemons, divided

¼ cup grated Parmesan cheese

½ cup chopped almonds

Zest of 1 lemon

1 cup chopped fresh basil

4 cups cooked brown rice, cooked according to package directions

Place chicken breasts on a baking sheet, and sprinkle with the juice of 1 lemon. Bake at 350° about 45 minutes or until done (at least 165° internal temperature). Remove from oven, and cut into bite-sized pieces.

Mix remaining ingredients together with cooked chicken in a large mixing bowl, and serve.

NUTRITIONAL DATA
Calories: 299
Total Fat: 9g
Saturated Fat: 2g
Trans Fat: 0g
Cholesterol: 49mg
Sodium: 101mg
Carbohydrates: 26g
Dietary Fiber: 3g
Sugars: 1g
Protein: 28g

Lemon and Asparagus Pasta

YIELD: 13 SERVINGS   SERVING SIZE: 1 CUP

2¼ pounds raw asparagus, sliced

Zest of 1 lemon

1 tablespoon dried tarragon

8 garlic cloves, chopped

2 large shallots, chopped

1 tablespoon olive oil

1 cup plain, nonfat Greek-style yogurt

Juice of 1 lemon

2 tablespoons chopped fresh parsley

¾ cup grated Parmesan cheese

½ cup low-sodium chicken broth, no sugar added

1 pound whole-grain pasta, cooked according to package directions

NUTRITIONAL DATA
Data does not include chicken.

Calories: 197	Sodium: 101mg
Total Fat: 4g	Carbohydrates: 31g
Saturated Fat: 1g	Dietary Fiber: 5g
Trans Fat: 0g	Sugars: 3g
Cholesterol: 5mg	Protein: 11g

Sauté asparagus, lemon zest, tarragon, garlic, and shallots in olive oil over low to medium heat. (The asparagus should be al dente, not mushy.) Combine all ingredients in a large mixing bowl, and serve while hot.

OPTIONAL FOR MEAT EATERS:

4 boneless skinless chicken breasts (about 7 ounces each)

Juice of 1 lemon

Zest of 1 lemon

If adding chicken, place chicken breasts on a parchment-lined cookie sheet topped with juice and zest. Bake at 350° about 45 minutes or until done (at least 165° internal temperature). Cut into bite-sized chunks, and stir in with other ingredients.

Carrot and Sun-Dried Tomato Penne

Carrot and Sun-Dried Tomato Penne

YIELD: 11 SERVINGS   SERVING SIZE: 1 CUP

2 garlic cloves, chopped

2 cups chopped red onions

3 cups sliced carrots

1 cup sun-dried tomatoes, drained, if packed in oil

1 tablespoon olive oil

1½ pounds lean ground turkey

½ pound whole-wheat penne pasta, cooked according to package directions

½ cup grated Parmesan cheese

Salt and pepper to taste

> **NUTRITIONAL DATA**
> Calories: 249
> Total Fat: 10g
> Saturated Fat: 3g
> Trans Fat: 0g
> Cholesterol: 53mg
> Sodium: 181mg
> Carbohydrates: 24g
> Dietary Fiber: 4g
> Sugars: 4g
> Protein: 17g

In a very large pan, sauté the garlic, onions, carrots, and sun-dried tomatoes in the olive oil for about 5 minutes. The onions should just start to wilt.

Add the turkey meat, and cook until completely cooked through (about 15 minutes).

Stir in the pasta, and remove from heat. Lastly, stir in the Parmesan cheese, and add salt and pepper to taste.

Parmesan Turkey with Brown Rice

YIELD: 8 SERVINGS   SERVING SIZE: 1 CUP

Brussels sprouts often get a bad rap in the flavor department, but prepared correctly, they impart a wonderful flavor to any dish. They also give you a wonderful supply of vitamins C and K.

1½ pounds lean ground turkey

1 tablespoon olive oil

1 pound Brussels sprouts, washed, trimmed, and cut in half

2 teaspoons garlic powder

2 teaspoons onion powder

2 tablespoons chopped fresh parsley

½ cup grated Parmesan cheese

NUTRITIONAL DATA
Data does not include rice.

Calories: 197

Total Fat: 11g

Saturated Fat: 3g

Trans Fat: 0g

Cholesterol: 73mg

Sodium: 191mg

Carbohydrates: 6g

Dietary Fiber: 2g

Sugars: 2g

Protein: 19g

In a large skillet, brown turkey in olive oil. Add Brussels sprouts, garlic powder, onion powder, and parsley, and continue to cook until the meat is completely cooked through. (Brussels sprouts should be al dente.) Stir in Parmesan just before serving. Serve over brown rice.

Turkey Cutlets with Quinoa Pilaf

YIELD: 4 SERVINGS   SERVING SIZE: 1 CUTLET AND 1 CUP QUINOA

Quinoa makes a delicious pilaf. We love quinoa for its versatility. Try this superfood as a dessert topping, breakfast, or as a side to the main dish. You can't go wrong with quinoa.

2 tablespoons canola oil, divided

1 shallot, thinly sliced

1 cup dry white quinoa, rinsed or pre-rinsed

2 cups fat-free, low-sodium chicken broth

1 bay leaf

½ cup frozen green peas, no added sugar

2 tablespoons diced pistachios

Sea salt to taste

Freshly ground black pepper to taste

4 (4-ounce) turkey cutlets

NUTRITIONAL DATA

Calories: 286	Sodium: 28mg
Total Fat: 10g	Carbohydrates: 33g
Saturated Fat: 1g	Dietary Fiber: 5g
Trans Fat: 0g	Sugars: 1g
Cholesterol: 18mg	Protein: 16g

In a medium saucepan, add 1 table-spoon canola oil, heat to medium-low, and sauté shallot slices until tender, about 5 minutes. Add dry quinoa, chicken broth, bay leaf, and green peas; stir. Bring to a boil, reduce heat to a simmer, cover, and cook 15 minutes or until liquid is absorbed. Remove bay leaf, and discard. Add sea salt and black pepper to taste. Add pistachios, allow to sit 5 minutes, then fluff with a fork, and serve with cutlets.

While pilaf is cooking, cook turkey cutlets. Add remaining canola oil to a large skillet, and heat to medium high. Season cutlets, add to skillet, and cook on each side until browned and crispy. Cover, and continue cooking on medium heat until turkey is cooked through and has an internal temperature of 165°. Serve turkey with pilaf as desired.

Smothered New York Strip Steak

YIELD: 3 SERVINGS   SERVING SIZE: 1 STEAK

Mushrooms have anti-inflammatory agents that may help boost the immune system and fight cancerous tumors. Almost any food can be made healthier by adding one or two superfoods. This steak is loaded with mushrooms and shallots.

2 tablespoons canola oil, divided

4 ounces white mushrooms, sliced

2 shallots, thinly sliced

1 tablespoon cornstarch

1 tablespoon balsamic vinegar

1 cup fat-free, low-sodium beef broth

Salt and pepper to taste

1 pound thin-cut New York strip steaks (recommend grass-fed beef)

NUTRITIONAL DATA

Calories: 292	Sodium: 165mg
Total Fat: 14g	Carbohydrates: 5g
Saturated Fat: 3g	Dietary Fiber: 0g
Trans Fat: 0g	Sugars: 1g
Cholesterol: 52mg	Protein: 34g

Add 1 tablespoon canola oil to a medium skillet, turn to medium-low heat, and sauté mushrooms and shallots until caramelized, about 10 minutes. Add cornstarch, and coat mushrooms and shallots; add balsamic vinegar and broth; stir, and turn to low heat until thickened. Salt and pepper to taste.

While sautéing, add remaining canola oil to a large skillet, heat to medium-high heat, and sear steaks on both sides, 8–10 minutes. Place steaks on a serving platter, and top with sauce.

Almond-Crusted Flounder

YIELD: 4 SERVINGS   SERVINGS: 1 FILLET

Enjoy a crunchy flounder fillet over a bed of baby spinach and fresh strawberries. You've probably heard, "fish is brain food." Fish is also low in saturated fat and sodium. The benefits don't stop there—it is an excellent source of vitamin B12, phosphorus, protein, selenium, and omega-3 fatty acids.

½ cup raw almonds

½ cup cornmeal

½ teaspoon cayenne pepper

½ teaspoon black pepper

4 flounder fillets (10 ounces)

1 large egg white, slightly beaten

2 tablespoons canola oil

Salt to taste

In a food processor, pulse almonds, cornmeal, cayenne, and black pepper until ingredients are combined and almonds are minced, while still having a slight amount of texture. Dip flounder fillets in egg white, then coat both sides with almond mixture. Using your hands, press coating onto fillets.

NUTRITIONAL DATA	
Calories: 361	Sodium: 162mg
Total Fat: 15g	Carbohydrates: 19g
Saturated Fat: 2g	Dietary Fiber: 2g
Trans Fat: 0g	Sugars: 1g
Cholesterol: 86mg	Protein: 36g

Add oil to a large skillet, on medium-high heat; sear fillets on both sides until golden and they easily flake with a fork. Remove from skillet, and pat with paper towels to remove excess oil. Season with salt to taste.

Wild Caught Cod with Couscous

Wild Caught Cod with Couscous

YIELD: 4 SERVINGS   SERVING SIZE: 1 FILLET

Cod provides a generous portion of heart-healthy omega-3's. This fish is high in niacin, magnesium, and phosphorus, and has an excellent source of protein and selenium.

½ cup fat-free, low-sodium chicken broth

2 teaspoons extra virgin olive oil

1 (10-ounce) can diced tomatoes with green chiles

1 tablespoon freshly squeezed lemon juice

¾ cup Mediterranean-style couscous (or use regular couscous)

Sea salt to taste

½ teaspoon freshly ground black pepper

4 (4-ounce) wild caught cod fillets

1 tablespoon canola oil

NUTRITIONAL DATA
Calories: 254
Total Fat: 9g
Saturated Fat: 1g
Trans Fat: 0g
Cholesterol: 46mg
Sodium: 216mg
Carbohydrates: 9g
Dietary Fiber: 1g
Sugars: 1g
Protein: 32g

In a medium saucepan, add chicken broth, olive oil, diced tomatoes, and lemon juice. Turn to medium-high heat, and bring to a boil; add couscous, salt, and pepper. Stir, cover saucepan, and remove from heat. Allow couscous to stand while preparing cod.

Season cod with additional salt and pepper, if desired. Add canola oil to a large nonstick skillet; cook fillets on medium high, until fillets flake with a fork, 2–3 minutes on each side. Remove from heat, and serve with couscous.

Blackened Wild Alaskan Salmon

YIELD: 2 SERVINGS   SERVING SIZE: ½ FILLET

Spice up dinner with this recipe that seals in flavor and has a crispy exterior. You can't beat salmon for its high protein content and heart-healthy omega-3 fatty acids.

1 (8-ounce) wild Alaskan salmon fillet

2 tablespoons extra virgin olive oil, divided

BLACKENED SEASONING:

½ teaspoon thyme

½ teaspoon garlic powder

½ teaspoon oregano

1 teaspoon paprika

½ teaspoon black pepper

½ teaspoon cayenne pepper

Salt to taste

Combine spices in a small bowl.

NUTRITIONAL DATA

Calories: 333	Sodium: 64mg
Total Fat: 23g	Carbohydrates: 2g
Saturated Fat: 3g	Dietary Fiber: 1g
Trans Fat: 0g	Sugars: 0g
Cholesterol: 80mg	Protein: 29g

Drizzle both sides of salmon with 1 tablespoon oil, and evenly coat both sides of salmon with Blackened Seasoning. Add remaining 1 tablespoon olive oil to a medium skillet, heat to medium high, and add salmon. Sear salmon 5–6 minutes on each side.

Honey-Dijon Glazed Salmon

YIELD: 2 SERVINGS   SERVING SIZE: ½ FILLET

One serving of this recipe boasts 29 grams of protein, and high amounts of vitamins B6 and B12, niacin, and selenium.

NUTRITIONAL DATA

Calories: 245	Sodium: 126mg
Total Fat: 9g	Carbohydrates: 9g
Saturated Fat: 1g	Dietary Fiber: 0g
Trans Fat: 0g	Sugars: 9g
Cholesterol: 80mg	Protein: 29g

1 tablespoon honey

1 tablespoon Dijon mustard

1 tablespoon freshly squeezed lemon juice

1 (8-ounce) wild Alaskan salmon fillet

Sea salt and pepper to taste

Combine honey, mustard, and lemon juice in a small bowl.

Line a rimmed cookie sheet with foil. Spread ¾ honey mixture over salmon, covering both sides. Season with salt and pepper to taste. Place salmon skin side down on cookie sheet; drizzle with remaining honey mixture. Place in oven 4–5 inches from broiler. Broil 4–5 minutes on each side or until cooked through. Serve on a bed of quinoa or brown rice.

Spinach Enchilada Solo

YIELD: 1 SERVING   SERVING SIZE: 1 ENCHILADA

This superfood recipe is for one but can easily be adapted for an entire family. Enjoy a Spinach Enchilada Solo, and don't worry, because the cholesterol is low and it's a great source of vitamins A and K. Spinach is known to contain cancer-fighting phytochemicals as well as beta carotene, iron, and folic acid.

1 ounce mushrooms, diced

1 tablespoon extra virgin olive oil

1 tablespoon diced onion

Salt and pepper to taste

¼ teaspoon crushed red pepper flakes

1 low-sodium whole-wheat tortilla

½ cup fresh baby spinach

⅓ cup fat-free cottage cheese

¼ cup verde sauce

1 romaine lettuce leaf, chopped

¼ cup diced tomato

1 tablespoon plain, nonfat Greek-style yogurt

NUTRITIONAL DATA	
Calories: 376	Sodium: 489mg
Total Fat: 18g	Carbohydrates: 72g
Saturated Fat: 3g	Dietary Fiber: 6g
Trans Fat: 0g	Sugars: 5g
Cholesterol: 8mg	Protein: 17g

Preheat oven to 375°.

In a medium skillet, sauté mushrooms in oil on medium heat until tender, about 8 minutes. Add onion, and continue sautéing another 3–4 minutes; sprinkle with salt, pepper, and red pepper flakes. Add to center of tortilla, the spinach, cottage cheese, mushrooms, and onion, leaving about 2 inches at the bottom for folding.

Spray a casserole dish with nonstick cooking spray. Fold stuffed tortilla lengthwise, and fold the one end under. Place seam side down in the casserole dish, then pour verde sauce over enchilada, and ensure the entire enchilada is moist. Cover, and bake 20–25 minutes. Top with chopped romaine, tomato, and yogurt.

Simple Garlicky Italian Fusilli

YIELD: 2 SERVINGS   SERVING SIZE: 1 CUP

This is an incredibly quick and simple dish to prepare. It gives you vitamins A, C, and K all wrapped up into a wonderful burst of flavor. For those who prefer their main meals with meat, this dish is wonderful with some chunks of baked chicken added.

2 garlic cloves, chopped

6 cups raw spinach leaves, packed tight when measuring

1 tablespoon olive oil

1 cup halved cherry tomatoes

½ pound whole-grain fusilli, cooked to package directions

Freshly chopped basil and grated Parmesan cheese for garnish

Sauté the garlic and spinach in the olive oil until the spinach is wilted. Remove the pan from heat, and stir in tomatoes and pasta. Top with chopped basil and Parmesan cheese.

NUTRITIONAL DATA
Data for pasta not included.

Calories: 94	Sodium: 18mg
Total Fat: 7g	Carbohydrates: 7g
Saturated Fat: 1g	Dietary Fiber: 1g
Trans Fat: 0g	Sugars: 2g
Cholesterol: 0mg	Protein: 2g

Note: Pasta varies in nutritional data, depending on what brand you buy. So that data is not included here. This is for the spinach topping only.

Super Veggie Lasagna

Super Veggie Lasagna

YIELD: 12 SERVINGS   SERVING SIZE: ½2 OF THE LASAGNA

3 cups grated carrots

2 cups grated zucchini

3 cups frozen spinach

1 medium bell pepper, chopped (any color)

3¼ cups diced fresh tomatoes

2 (15-ounce) cans tomato sauce, no salt added
  (we used Hunt's brand)

1 teaspoon oregano

2 teaspoons dried basil

2 teaspoons onion powder

2 teaspoons garlic powder

½ pound brown mushrooms

1 (12-ounce) package whole-wheat lasagna
  noodles, cooked to package directions

1½ cups grated Parmesan cheese, divided

8 ounces grated mozzarella (2 cups)

Chopped fresh basil for garnish (optional)

NUTRITIONAL DATA
Calories: 279
Total Fat: 8g
Saturated Fat: 4g
Trans Fat: 0g
Cholesterol: 23mg
Sodium: 384mg
Carbohydrates: 37g
Dietary Fiber: 7g
Sugars: 9g
Protein: 17g

Combine all ingredients, except the noodles and chees-es, in a large mixing bowl. Stir well to combine.

Layer in a lightly greased 9x13-inch baking dish: noodles, ½ cup Parmesan cheese, ½ the veggie mix, noodles, ½ cup Parmesan cheese, remaining veggie mix, noodles, remaining Parmesan cheese, and all the mozzarella. Bake at 350° for 40 minutes. Garnish with a bit of fresh, chopped basil, if desired.

Mediterranean Penne

YIELD: 5 SERVINGS   SERVING SIZE: 1 CUP

This penne recipe is low in saturated fat, and very low in cholesterol. It is also a good source of vitamin A, which helps to improve night vision and is an immune booster.

5 cups cooked whole-grain penne pasta, cooked al dente

2 tablespoons extra virgin olive oil, divided

2 garlic cloves, minced

¾ cup sun-dried tomatoes, coarsely chopped

½ teaspoon black pepper

Salt to taste

½ teaspoon crushed red pepper flakes

½ cup pine nuts

2 cups baby spinach

1 cup fat-free feta cheese

NUTRITIONAL DATA	
Calories: 318	Sodium: 389mg
Total Fat: 13g	Carbohydrates: 41g
Saturated Fat: 1g	Dietary Fiber: 6g
Trans Fat: 0g	Sugars: 5g
Cholesterol: 4mg	Protein: 11g

Cook penne according to package directions. Add 1 tablespoon extra virgin olive oil to a large skillet, and sauté garlic over medium-low heat until fragrant, about 1 minute. Add to skillet the sun-dried tomatoes, black pepper, salt, and red pepper flakes, and continue cooking 5 minutes or until tomatoes are soft. Add cooked penne and remaining tablespoon of oil; toss to coat, cover, and cook on low an additional 2 minutes. Add pine nuts and baby spinach; combine; cook just until spinach is slightly wilted, about 1 minute.

Serve topped with feta cheese.

Purple Stir-Fry

YIELD: 6 SERVINGS   SERVING SIZE: 1 CUP

We love stir-fry. Even more so when that stir-fry is purple! It's a fantastic way to get a big serving of vegetables, fiber, and nutrients in one delicious dish. It's a veritable buffet of vitamins such as A, C, K, B6, and many more.

4 cups chopped red cabbage
½ cup peeled and sliced carrots
2 cups chopped zucchini
1 cup chopped red bell peppers
2 cups sliced mushrooms
¾ cups vegetable broth, no sugar added
2 teaspoons garlic powder
2 teaspoons onion powder

In a large skillet, combine all ingredients, and cook until vegetables are tender, or to your liking. Serve over brown rice or quinoa with a dash of soy sauce.

NUTRITIONAL DATA
Calories: 50
Total Fat: 0g
Saturated Fat: 0g
Trans Fat: 0g
Cholesterol: 0mg
Sodium: 71mg
Carbohydrates: 11g
Dietary Fiber: 3g
Sugars: 5g
Protein: 3g

Curried Quinoa with Chickpeas

YIELD: 4½ SERVINGS   SERVING SIZE: 1 CUP

This is a great dish when you have some extra, left-over quinoa. But whether you cook the quinoa or use leftovers, this dish is simple and comes together quickly. It can be served as a vegetarian dish, or simply add some baked chicken for a delicious and complete dinner. Great for those busy weeknights!

2 cups cooked quinoa

1 cup grated carrots

1 cup chopped tomatoes

1½ cups cooked or canned chickpeas (garbanzo beans)

2 teaspoons curry powder

2 teaspoons garlic powder

1 teaspoon onion powder

Salt to taste

In a large mixing bowl, combine all ingredients, and mix well.

NUTRITIONAL DATA
Sodium will be higher if using canned beans.

Calories: 216

Total Fat: 4g

Saturated Fat: 0g

Trans Fat: 0g

Cholesterol: 0mg

Sodium: 30mg

Carbohydrates: 38g

Dietary Fiber: 8g

Sugars: 6g

Protein: 10g

Broccoli Quinoa Stir-Fry

YIELD: 9 SERVINGS   SERVING SIZE: 1 CUP

Quinoa is an amazing seed that is cooked and eaten as a grain. It offers a wonderful variety to your diet and is incredibly versatile. It's also a good way to get magnesium and manganese into your daily eating plan.

4 cups raw chopped broccoli

2 tablespoons sesame or olive oil

2 teaspoons garlic powder

1 teaspoon onion powder

2 tablespoons sesame seeds

4 egg whites, or 1 whole egg and 2 egg whites, beaten

2 cups cooked quinoa

Low-sodium soy sauce to taste

Sauté the broccoli in the oil until it becomes just slightly soft. Stir in the garlic powder, onion powder, sesame seeds, and eggs, and cook over medium heat until eggs are fully cooked. Add the quinoa, and stir well to combine. Add soy sauce to taste, and serve.

NUTRITIONAL DATA
Data reflects using 4 egg whites.
Calories: 117
Total Fat: 5g
Saturated Fat: 1g
Trans Fat: 0g
Cholesterol: 0mg
Sodium: 41mg
Carbohydrates: 13g
Dietary Fiber: 3g
Sugars: 1g
Protein: 5g

Bok Choy and Quinoa Stir-Fry

Bok Choy and Quinoa Stir-Fry

YIELD: 4 SERVINGS   SERVING SIZE: 1 CUP

This recipe is packed with cancer-fighting phytochemicals, vitamins, and minerals. Broccolini, which is a cross between broccoli and Chinese kale, is sweet and tender while still having a broccoli taste. These superfoods are very low in cholesterol, and are good sources of vitamins A and C, folate, phosphorus, copper, and protein.

1 tablespoon extra virgin olive oil

1 teaspoon sesame seed oil

2 garlic cloves, minced

3 stalks Bok Choy, leaves removed, sliced into ½-inch pieces

6 Broccolini

¼ cup roasted sesame seeds, no salt added

1 tablespoon lite soy sauce

2 cups cooked white quinoa, cook according instructions on package

Salt to taste

NUTRITIONAL DATA
Calories: 250
Total Fat: 13g
Saturated Fat: 2g
Trans Fat: 0g
Cholesterol: 0mg
Sodium: 182mg
Carbohydrates: 28g
Dietary Fiber: 5g
Sugars: 1g
Protein: 9g

In a large skillet, add oils, turn to medium-low heat, and sauté garlic until fragrant, about 1 minute. Add Bok Choy and Broccolini, cover, and continue cooking 6 minutes. Add sesame seeds, soy sauce, and quinoa; stir, cover, and cook an additional 2 minutes.

Curried Lentils

YIELD: 8 SERVINGS   SERVING SIZE: 1 CUP

Get half the day's fiber requirement in just one cup of this delicious recipe. You'll also get vitamins B6, A, and K while you enjoy a wonderfully comforting dish.

2 cups dry lentils

7 cups low-sodium vegetable broth, no sugar added

2 cups sliced carrots

2 cups chopped celery

1 tablespoon curry powder, or to taste

2 teaspoons ground cinnamon

1 teaspoon ground cumin

2 teaspoons garlic powder

2 teaspoons onion powder

½ teaspoon ground ginger

3 cups fresh spinach, packed tight when measuring

1 tablespoon balsamic vinegar

1½ cups lite coconut milk

6 garlic cloves, chopped

2 cups grated zucchini

Combine all ingredients in a large soup pot, and bring to a boil. Reduce to a gentle boil, and cook until all the liquid has been absorbed and the lentils are soft.

NUTRITIONAL DATA
Sodium content will vary greatly depending on broth used.

Calories: 241	Sodium: 367mg
Total Fat: 4g	Carbohydrates: 38g
Saturated Fat: 2g	Dietary Fiber: 17g
Trans Fat: 0g	Sugars: 5g
Cholesterol: 0mg	Protein: 15g

Note: If you find that the liquid cooks out before the lentils are fully cooked, simply add water or more broth, one cup at a time, until lentils are fully cooked.

Southwestern Black Bean Casserole

YIELD: 6 SERVINGS   SERVING SIZE: 1 CUP

Legumes are an excellent source of protein and are often eaten in vegetarian diets as an option to animal protein.

2 (15-ounce) cans black beans, drained

2 teaspoons extra virgin olive oil

2 garlic cloves, minced

½ cup fat-free, low-sodium vegetable broth

1 teaspoon cumin

¼ teaspoon black pepper

Salt to taste

2 tablespoons chopped fresh cilantro

4 low-sodium whole-wheat tortillas

12 ounces salsa, no added sugar

1 cup shredded 2% Cheddar cheese

NUTRITIONAL DATA	
Calories: 259	Sodium: 436mg
Total Fat: 5g	Carbohydrates: 40g
Saturated Fat: 2g	Dietary Fiber: 9g
Trans Fat: 0g	Sugars: 4g
Cholesterol: 4mg	Protein: 12g

Preheat oven to 375°. Drain beans, and set aside. In the meantime, in a medium skillet, add oil; heat over medium-low heat. Add garlic, and sauté until tender, about 4 minutes. Add black beans and broth, and continue cooking approximately 3 minutes. Add cumin, black pepper, salt, and cilantro; stir to combine.

Spray the bottom of an 8x8-inch casserole dish with nonstick cooking spray. Add a tortilla, ¼ black bean mixture, ¼ salsa, and ¼ cheese; continue layering until all ingredients have been used. Top casserole with remaining ¼ cup cheese.

Cover casserole dish with foil, and bake approximately 20 minutes or until cheese is hot and bubbly. Remove foil, and continue cooking 8–10 minutes. Remove from oven, and garnish with sour cream, if desired.

Crustless Vegetable Quiche

YIELD: 6 SERVINGS   SERVING SIZE: 1 SLICE

Enjoy this dish as a main course or for breakfast. This recipe is a good source of protein, vitamins A and C, riboflavin, calcium, phosphorus, and selenium. All and all, this recipe is packed with disease-fighting antioxidants.

1 tablespoon olive oil

1 small yellow onion, diced

2 garlic cloves, minced

½ cup diced red bell pepper

½ cup diced green bell pepper

½ cup sliced zucchini

6 Broccolini, leaves removed, chopped (optional, broccoli florets)

¼ cup diced sun-dried tomatoes, packed in oil

2 large eggs

5 large egg whites

2 tablespoons low-fat milk

1 teaspoon dried oregano

½ teaspoon black pepper

Sea salt to taste

¼ cup plus 1 tablespoon low-fat Parmesan cheese, divided

NUTRITIONAL DATA	
Calories: 121	Sodium: 311mg
Total Fat: 7g	Carbohydrates: 6g
Saturated Fat: 3g	Dietary Fiber: 1g
Trans Fat: 0g	Sugars: 3g
Cholesterol: 83mg	Protein: 9g

spray a 9-inch pie plate or sauté pan with nonstick cooking spray; add sautéed vegetables. Pour egg mixture over vegetables; make sure to cover all veggies. Loosely cover with foil, and bake 10 minutes at 425°. Reduce heat to 350°, and continue baking 20–25 minutes. Remove foil the last few minutes of baking time, and sprinkle with the remaining Parmesan cheese. Quiche is done when it puffs and a knife inserted in the center comes out clean.

Preheat oven to 425°.

In a large skillet on medium-low heat, add oil, and sauté onion and garlic until tender, about 4 minutes. Add diced bell peppers, zucchini, broccolini, and sun-dried tomatoes; continue sautéing 2 minutes.

In a medium mixing bowl, whisk together eggs, egg whites, milk, spices, and ¼ cup Parmesan cheese. Lightly

Sweets and Treats

Maple Flax and Cranberry Muffins

Maple Flax and Cranberry Muffins

YIELD: 12 SERVINGS   SERVING SIZE: 2 MUFFINS

These low-sodium, no-cholesterol muffins are sure to delight your pickiest eaters with all whole-food ingredients.

2 cups white whole-wheat flour

2 teaspoons baking powder

½ teaspoon cinnamon

1 teaspoon ground allspice

1 cup dried cranberries

2 egg whites

1 cup unsweetened almond milk (or 1% milk)

1 cup maple syrup

1 teaspoon vanilla extract

3 tablespoons coconut oil (or other healthy oil)

1 cup unsweetened applesauce

½ cup flax seeds

NUTRITIONAL DATA
Calories: 251
Total Fat: 7g
Saturated Fat: 3g
Trans Fat: 0g
Cholesterol: 0mg
Sodium: 110mg
Carbohydrates: 46g
Dietary Fiber: 5g
Sugars: 25g
Protein: 5g

In a large mixing bowl, whisk together the flour, baking powder, cinnamon, allspice, and cranberries. In a medium mixing bowl, whisk together the rest of the ingredients. Combine the 2 bowls into the larger bowl, and stir well. Portion out the batter into 24 foil baking cups held in a muffin tin, or use a nonstick muffin tin. Bake at 350° for 40 minutes or until the muffins are baked through. Allow to cool, and serve.

Note: You'll want to use foil baking cups, as these muffins will stick to the paper variety.

Super Fruit Muffins

YIELD: 11 SERVINGS   SERVING SIZE: 2 MUFFINS

Get all the good nutrition that healthy fruits can give you while enjoying this wonderful treat in moderation. Low in sodium, these muffins are a tasty way to add some selenium and manganese to your daily nutrition intake.

2 cups white whole-wheat flour

2 teaspoons baking powder

1 teaspoon cinnamon

2 egg whites

1 cup fat-free milk

¾ cup honey

2 teaspoons vanilla extract

2 tablespoons coconut oil (or other healthy oil)

1 small banana, mashed

1 cup grated apple (about one medium apple)

2 cups fresh blueberries

NUTRITIONAL DATA	
Calories: 209	Sodium: 109mg
Total Fat: 3g	Carbohydrates: 44g
Saturated Fat: 0g	Dietary Fiber: 4g
Trans Fat: 0g	Sugars: 25g
Cholesterol: 0mg	Protein: 5g

Mix together the flour, baking powder, and cinnamon in a large mixing bowl. Add in egg whites, milk, honey, vanilla extract, coconut oil, and banana. Thoroughly combine the 2 mixtures into the larger bowl, then gently stir in the grated apple and blueberries. Portion the batter into 22 foil baking cups or a nonstick muffin tin, and bake at 350° for about 40 minutes.

Note: You'll want to use foil baking cups, as these muffins will stick to the paper variety.

Cherry Almond Muffins

YIELD: 12 SERVINGS   SERVING SIZE: 2 MUFFINS

Who says muffins can't be healthy? Enjoy these in moderation for a wonderful, tasty snack or dessert.

2 cups white whole-wheat flour

2 teaspoons baking powder

¼ cup chopped almonds

2 tablespoons flax seeds

3 egg whites

1 cup fat-free milk

¾ cup honey

2 teaspoons almond extract

2 tablespoons safflower oil (or other healthy oil)

1 cup unsweetened applesauce

1 (12-ounce) bag frozen, unsweetened cherries, thawed slightly

NUTRITIONAL DATA	
Calories: 196	Sodium: 105mg
Total Fat: 4g	Carbohydrates: 37g
Saturated Fat: 0g	Dietary Fiber: 4g
Trans Fat: 0g	Sugars: 21g
Cholesterol: 0mg	Protein: 5g

Combine the flour, baking powder, almonds, and flax seeds in a large mixing bowl. In a medium mixing bowl, combine the egg whites, milk, honey, almond extract, oil, and applesauce. Stir the wet ingredients into the flour mixture, and stir well to combine. Fold in cherries. Portion the batter into 12 foil baking cups or a nonstick muffin tin, and bake at 350° for about 40 minutes.

Note: You'll want to use foil baking cups, as these muffins will stick to the paper variety.

Banana Walnut Bread

YIELD: 12 SERVINGS   SERVING SIZE: ¹⁄₁₂ OF RECIPE

Bananas, coconut oil, and yogurt make this traditional dessert bread moist and delicious. Enjoy a slice, and reap the benefits of calcium, which helps to prevent osteoporosis, bananas which protect against anemia, and vitamin A which supports a healthy immune system.

⅓ cup coconut oil, melted (extra virgin recommended)

¾ cup honey

1 egg

1 cup well-mashed bananas, about 2 bananas (very ripe is best)

½ cup plain, nonfat Greek-style yogurt

1 teaspoon pure vanilla extract

1½ cups white whole-wheat flour

¼ teaspoon salt

1 teaspoon baking soda

1 teaspoon cinnamon

1 cup chopped walnuts

NUTRITIONAL DATA	
Calories: 289	Sodium: 18g
Total Fat: 13g	Carbohydrates: 37g
Saturated Fat: 6g	Dietary Fiber: 4g
Trans Fat: 0g	Sugars: 19g
Cholesterol: 18g	Protein: 7g

Preheat oven to 325°.

In a large mixing bowl, on medium speed, cream together coconut oil and honey. Add egg, mashed bananas, yogurt, and vanilla; mix until combined, 1–2 minutes. Whisk together in a small bowl, the flour, salt, baking soda, and cinnamon. Fold flour mixture into wet batter, stirring just until moistened. Stir in nuts.

Pour batter into 5x9-inch loaf pan coated with cooking spray. Bake 55–60 minutes or until a fork or toothpick inserted in center comes out clean. Cool 15 minutes in pan before removing, then cool completely on a wire rack.

Note: To reduce fat content, omit nuts.

Oatmeal Carrot Banana Nut Cookies

YIELD: 12 SERVINGS   SERVING SIZE: 2 COOKIES

Who would have thought that a cookie could be a good source of vitamin A? Just one serving of these cookies will give you approximately 30% of the daily recommended amount (based on a 2,000-calorie diet). Enjoy in moderation, but enjoy!

1½ cups quick-cooking oats

1 cup white whole-wheat flour

1 teaspoon cinnamon

¼ teaspoon salt

1 teaspoon baking powder

½ cup chopped pecans

2 medium-size ripe bananas, mashed

¼ cup coconut oil

2 egg whites

⅓ cup honey

2 teaspoons vanilla

1 cup grated carrots

NUTRITIONAL DATA

Calories: 170	Sodium: 91mg
Total Fat: 8g	Carbohydrates: 24g
Saturated Fat: 4g	Dietary Fiber: 3g
Trans Fat: 0g	Sugars: 9g
Cholesterol: 0mg	Protein: 3g

Combine the oats, flour, cinnamon, salt, baking powder, and pecans in a large mixing bowl. Combine the bananas, oil, egg whites, honey, vanilla, and carrots in a medium mixing bowl. Pour the wet ingredients into the flour mix, and stir with a large wooden spoon to combine. Scoop 24 cookies onto parchment-lined cookie sheets, and bake at 350° for about 12 minutes, or until the cookies are baked through.

Note: If these cookies seem hard after baking, simply pack them away overnight in a plastic bag, and they will be quite soft in the morning.

Hearty Oatmeal Raisin Cookies

Hearty Oatmeal Raisin Cookies

YIELD: 8 SERVINGS   SERVING SIZE: 2 COOKIES

These robust cookies are not your typical cookie that you can swallow in one bite and then move on to the next. You <u>know</u> you've eaten a cookie when you're done with one of these bad boys. Plus, they have no cholesterol and are a good way to get some manganese into your eating plan. Enjoy in moderation; these are definitely a treat.

1 cup white whole-wheat flour

1 cup quick-cooking oats (3-minute variety)

2 teaspoons baking powder

1 teaspoon cinnamon

1 cup raisins

2 tablespoons coconut oil (or other healthy oil, such as safflower)

3 egg whites

2 teaspoons pure vanilla extract

½ cup honey

NUTRITIONAL DATA
Calories: 255
Total Fat: 4g
Saturated Fat: 3g
Trans Fat: 0g
Cholesterol: 0mg
Sodium: 144mg
Carbohydrates: 52g
Dietary Fiber: 4g
Sugars: 30g
Protein: 5g

In a large mixing bowl, combine all dry ingredients. In a medium mixing bowl, combine the wet ingredients. Pour the wet ingredients into the bowl with the dry mix, and blend well with a wooden spoon. Portion out 16 cookies onto parchment-lined cookie sheets. Bake at 350° for 15 minutes, or until just golden brown.

Note: If these cookies seem hard after baking, simply pack them away overnight in a plastic bag, and they will be quite soft in the morning.

Oatmeal Zucchini Cookies with Dark Chocolate Chunks

YIELD: 12 SERVINGS   SERVING SIZE: 2 COOKIES

It's nice to know that while you are enjoying a no-cholesterol, low-sodium cookie, you are also getting some iron and calcium. Enjoy these cookies in moderation, but do enjoy them. We all need a treat every now and then.

1 cup white whole-wheat flour

1½ cups quick-cooking oats

1 teaspoon baking powder

1 teaspoon cinnamon

¼ teaspoon salt

½ cup unsweetened applesauce

¼ cup coconut oil

2 egg whites

½ cup honey

1 teaspoon vanilla

1 cup grated zucchini

1 cup chopped dark chocolate

NUTRITIONAL DATA	
Calories: 237	Sodium: 89mg
Total Fat: 11g	Carbohydrates: 31g
Saturated Fat: 7g	Dietary Fiber: 4g
Trans Fat: 0g	Sugars: 15g
Cholesterol: 0mg	Protein: 4g

Combine dry ingredients in a large mixing bowl, and whisk to blend. Combine remaining ingredients in a medium mixing bowl, and whisk well to combine. Mix wet ingredients and dry ingredients with a wooden spoon until well blended. Scoop 24 equal portions of dough onto a parchment-lined cookie sheet. Bake at 350° for approximately 12 minutes, or until the cookies just begin to turn golden brown.

Sweet Potato Oatmeal Cookies

YIELD: 9 SERVINGS   SERVING SIZE: 2 COOKIES

Eaten in moderation, these cookies will give you approximately 85% of your daily recommended allowance of vitamin A (based on a 2,000-calorie diet). They are low in sodium and saturated fat, and have no cholesterol. Pretty good for a cookie!

1 cup white whole-wheat flour

1½ cups quick-cooking oats

1 teaspoon baking powder

1 teaspoon cinnamon

½ teaspoon allspice

1 cup cooked mashed sweet potatoes

¼ cup safflower oil

2 egg whites

½ cup honey

1 teaspoon vanilla

Combine all dry ingredients in a large mixing bowl. Combine all wet ingredients in a medium mixing bowl. Combine wet and dry ingredients in the larger of the 2 mixing bowls, and stir well to combine. Spoon 18 equal portions of cookie dough onto parchment-lined cookie sheets, and bake at 350° for 18–20 minutes, or until the cookies are fully baked. Allow to cool, and serve.

Note: If these cookies seem hard after baking, simply pack them away overnight in a plastic bag, and they will be quite soft in the morning.

NUTRITIONAL DATA	
Calories: 233	Sodium: 75mg
Total Fat: 7g	Carbohydrates: 40g
Saturated Fat: 1g	Dietary Fiber: 4g
Trans Fat: 0g	Sugars: 17g
Cholesterol: 0mg	Protein: 5g

Blood Oranges with Walnuts

YIELD: 4 SERVINGS   SERVING SIZE: 1 ORANGE, 1 TABLESPOON WALNUTS

This sweet and savory dessert is so simple to make, yet makes an elegant dish. You can enjoy every bite knowing this treat is low in cholesterol and sodium, and a good source of dietary fiber and vitamin C.

2 tablespoons honey
2 tablespoons water
½ teaspoon cinnamon
½ teaspoon pure vanilla extract
4 blood oranges, cut into segments, peelings and seeds removed
¼ cup diced walnuts

NUTRITIONAL DATA

Calories: 147	Sodium: 1g
Total Fat: 5g	Carbohydrates: 26g
Saturated Fat: 0g	Dietary Fiber: 4g
Trans Fat: 0g	Sugars: 22g
Cholesterol: 0g	Protein: 2g

Combine honey, water, cinnamon, and vanilla in a small bowl. In a medium skillet, heat to medium low; add orange wedges, honey mixture, and walnuts, and toss to coat. Cover, reduce heat to low, and warm oranges until honey thickens, 4–6 minutes. Serve warm in dessert dishes, drizzled with syrup.

Strawberry Mango Fruit Salad

YIELD: 2 SERVINGS   SERVING SIZE: 1 CUP

Who can argue with a delicious fruit salad for dessert? This light, summertime delight will leave you feeling satisfied, without having to unbutton your jeans.

1 cup chopped strawberries
1 cup chopped mango
Juice of 1 large lime
2 tablespoons chopped fresh mint

NUTRITIONAL DATA

Calories: 88	Sodium: 5mg
Total Fat: 1g	Carbohydrates: 23g
Saturated Fat: 0g	Dietary Fiber: 4g
Trans Fat: 0g	Sugars: 17g
Cholesterol: 0mg	Protein: 1g

Combine all ingredients well, and serve.

Stuffed Strawberries

YIELD: 12 SERVINGS   SERVING SIZE: 4 STUFFED BERRIES

Enjoy some vitamin C with your dessert. One serving of these berries will give you approximately 74% of your daily recommended amount (based on a 2,000-calorie diet). What a delicious way to enjoy summertime strawberries.

48 large strawberries
1½ cups dark chocolate (optional)
1 cup low-fat cottage cheese
¼ cup honey
2 tablespoons lemon zest
1 tablespoon lemon juice

Cut the stems off the strawberries, and a small amount of the ends as well, so that the strawberries stand up on their skinny end. Hollow out the insides. Place all strawberries on a paper towel, and allow the juices to seep out onto the paper towel as needed.

If desired, dip the tips of strawberries in melted chocolate. Set the strawberries upright (small side dipped in chocolate) on a parchment-lined cookie sheet, and place in refrigerator to cool.

In a blender, blend together the cottage cheese, honey, lemon zest, and lemon juice until smooth. Place filling in a plastic sandwich bag; cut off a small piece of a corner, and use like a cake bag to fill the strawberries. Keep in refrigerator until ready to serve.

Note: It's best to fill these as close to serving time as possible. If not using chocolate, set the strawberries on a paper towel, as the berries will lose some juice as they sit.

NUTRITIONAL DATA	
Data does not include chocolate.	
Calories: 62	Sodium: 66mg
Total Fat: 1g	Carbohydrates: 12g
Saturated Fat: 0g	Dietary Fiber: 1g
Trans Fat: 0g	Sugars: 10g
Cholesterol: 2mg	Protein: 3g

Coconut Banana Cream Pudding

Coconut Banana Cream Pudding

YIELD: 4 SERVINGS   SERVING SIZE: ½ CUP

This pudding is ultra rich and creamy and filled with superfood benefits. Both coconut milk and bananas are good sources of antioxidants and potassium. Coconut milk also has the added benefit of calcium and magnesium.

¼ cup cornstarch
¼ teaspoon salt
⅓ cup honey
2 egg yolks, slightly beaten
1½ cups lite coconut milk, canned
½ cup coconut flakes
1 teaspoon vanilla extract
2 bananas, sliced into ½-inch pieces

NUTRITIONAL DATA
Calories: 227
Total Fat: 10g
Saturated Fat: 8g
Trans Fat: 0g
Cholesterol: 60g
Sodium: 102g
Carbohydrates: 36g
Dietary Fiber: 2g
Sugars: 25g
Protein: 3g

In a heavy saucepan, mix cornstarch and salt. Add honey and egg yolks to dry ingredients; gradually stir in milk until well combined. Cook over medium heat while stirring continuously to prevent sticking. Cook until desired thickness, 8–10 minutes.

Remove from heat, and add coconut and vanilla extract; stir. Allow to cool about 15 minutes. Serve in individual dessert dishes topped with sliced bananas. This pudding is best served slightly warm. Refrigerate any unused portions.

Tip: This recipe can either be used as a pudding or pie filling. For an eye-pleasing garnish, add a sprinkle of coconut.

Bittersweet-Chocolate Pudding

YIELD: 6 SERVINGS   SERVING SIZE: ½ CUP

This mouthwatering pudding will impress the most discerning dinner guests. This recipe is low in both cholesterol and sodium. Dark chocolate has antioxidant properties that support a healthy immune system.

¼ cup cornstarch
¼ teaspoon salt
¼ cup honey
1½ cups lite coconut milk, canned
1½ cups 2% milk
1 cup bittersweet-chocolate chips
1 tablespoon orange zest
1 teaspoon vanilla extract

In a heavy saucepan, mix cornstarch and salt. Add honey, milks, chocolate chips, and orange zest; stir until well combined.

Cook over medium-low heat while stirring continuously to prevent sticking. Cook until desired thickness, about 15 minutes. Remove from heat, stir in vanilla, and allow to cool. As a garnish, top pudding with roasted minced almonds and additional orange zest.

NUTRITIONAL DATA	
Calories: 283	Sodium: 121g
Total Fat: 17g	Carbohydrates: 36g
Saturated Fat: 11g	Dietary Fiber: 2g
Trans Fat: 0g	Sugars: 25g
Cholesterol: 2g	Protein: 5g

Note: To roast almonds, preheat oven to 325°; place 1 cup raw almonds on parchment paper, and roast 12–13 minutes. Allow almonds to cool completely, place in food processor, and pulse until minced. This added touch has the taste and texture of a cookie when served over Bittersweet-Chocolate Pudding.

Tip: This recipe can either be used as a pudding or pie filling.

Quinoa Berry Parfait

YIELD: 2 SERVINGS   SERVING SIZE: 1 CUP

Thought by most to be a grain, quinoa is actually a seed. Quinoa is a gluten-free food and is high in protein, dietary fiber, and vitamin C.

½ cup plain, nonfat Greek-style yogurt

2 teaspoons honey

1 teaspoon freshly squeezed lemon juice

½ cup fresh blackberries

½ cup fresh raspberries

½ cup Quinoa Crisp

Combine yogurt, honey, and lemon juice in a small mixing bowl. Cover, and refrigerate until ready to use.

Layer half of berries, yogurt, and Quinoa Crisp in parfait dessert dishes, and repeat.

NUTRITIONAL DATA	
Calories: 139	Sodium: 32g
Total Fat: 1g	Carbohydrates: 26g
Saturated Fat: 0g	Dietary Fiber: 5g
Trans Fat: 0g	Sugars: 17g
Cholesterol: 2g	Protein: 8g

QUINOA CRISP:

¼ cup red quinoa (rinse according to package directions)

½ cup water

2 teaspoons honey

Add quinoa and water to a small pot, bring to a boil over medium-high heat, cover, and reduce to a simmer. Cook quinoa for 15 minutes, or until all water is absorbed. Add honey, and stir. Allow quinoa to cool while oven preheats to 325°.

Line a cookie sheet with parchment paper, spread quinoa evenly, and place in preheated oven. Stir quinoa after 15 minutes, and continue cooking 10 additional minutes.

Tip: Add Quinoa Crisp to yogurt, cereal, or granola, or eat as a stand-alone snack.

Cherry Compote for Parfaits

YIELD: 2 SERVINGS   SERVING SIZE: ½ THE RECIPE

Dessert can really pack on the sugar and calories, so why not ensure that those sugars are, at the very least, natural sugars? This no-cholesterol, low-sodium treat gives you 19% of your daily requirement for vitamin A as well. Can't say that for most desserts!

1 cup pitted fresh cherries (unsweetened frozen works as well)

1 cup water

3 tablespoons honey (or to taste, after cooking)

NUTRITIONAL DATA

Calories: 144
Total Fat: 0g
Saturated Fat: 0g
Trans Fat: 0g
Cholesterol: 0mg
Sodium: 1mg
Carbohydrates: 38g
Dietary Fiber: 2g
Sugars: 36g
Protein: 1g

Bring all ingredients to a boil in a small pot, then reduce heat to a simmer. Continue cooking until the mixture has reduced by at least half and the liquid is more like syrup. Cool, and serve with plain, nonfat Greek-style yogurt and a healthy granola or chopped nuts of your choice.

Note: Nutritional data is for Cherry Compote only and does not include yogurt, granola, or nuts.

Cherry Yogurt with Pistachios

YIELD: 2 SERVINGS   SERVING SIZE: ¾ CUP

In this deliciously light dish, Greek-style yogurt pairs up with cherries and pistachios to offer a wonderful, healthy, and easy dessert.

1 cup plain, nonfat Greek-style yogurt

2 tablespoons honey (or to taste)

½ cup chopped, pitted cherries

2 tablespoons shelled pistachios, no salt added

NUTRITIONAL DATA	
Calories: 228	Sodium: 37mg
Total Fat: 7g	Carbohydrates: 31g
Saturated Fat: 1g	Dietary Fiber: 2g
Trans Fat: 0g	Sugars: 26g
Cholesterol: 0mg	Protein: 14g

Mix all ingredients together, and serve.

Blackberry-Banana Ice Cream

YIELD: 3 SERVINGS   SERVING SIZE: 1 CUP

The rich purple color of blackberries is the result of flavonoids, which may help in the fight against cancer and heart disease. This healthy combination is a good source of dietary fiber and vitamin B6.

2 frozen bananas, sliced into ¼-inch pieces before freezing

1 cup frozen blackberries

1 tablespoon wheat germ

2 tablespoons honey

½ cup milk

NUTRITIONAL DATA	
Calories: 188	Sodium: 19g
Total Fat: 2g	Carbohydrates: 42g
Saturated Fat: 1g	Dietary Fiber: 5g
Trans Fat: 0g	Sugars: 29g
Cholesterol: 6g	Protein: 4g

Add all ingredients to a food processor; pulse until blended and creamy. This process requires stopping and stirring a few times and may take 2–3 minutes to fully blend ingredients.

Serve ice cream immediately . . . do NOT freeze.

Strawberries in Yogurt Sauce

YIELD: 2 SERVINGS   SERVING SIZE: ⅔ CUP

The flavor combination of strawberries in yogurt with white balsamic vinegar is delicious. White balsamic vinegar has a milder, fruitier taste than regular balsamic vinegar, and pairs beautifully with dessert dishes. This dessert has the added health benefits derived from both yogurt and strawberries. The red beauties contain antioxidants that fight cancer, and are high in fiber, vitamin C, and vitamin E.

½ cup plain, nonfat Greek-style yogurt

1 tablespoon white balsamic vinegar

1 tablespoon honey

10 fresh strawberries, thinly sliced

In a small mixing bowl, combine yogurt, vinegar, and honey. In dessert dishes, layer strawberries and yogurt mixture; repeat for 3 layers.

NUTRITIONAL DATA	
Calories: 95	Sodium: 3g
Total Fat: 0g	Carbohydrates: 17g
Saturated Fat: 0g	Dietary Fiber: 1g
Trans Fat: 0g	Sugars: 15g
Cholesterol: 2g	Protein: 6g

Blackberry-Raspberry Mini Cobblers

YIELD: 6 SERVINGS   SERVING SIZE: ½ CUP

These mini cobblers are low in saturated fat, sodium, and cholesterol. More good news . . . they are also a good source of dietary fiber and vitamin C.

4 cups frozen blackberries

2 cups frozen raspberries

⅓ cup honey

2 tablespoons freshly squeezed lemon juice

2 tablespoons cornstarch

NUTRITIONAL DATA

Calories: 257	Sodium: 91g
Total Fat: 6g	Carbohydrates: 47g
Saturated Fat: 0g	Dietary Fiber: 8g
Trans Fat: 0g	Sugars: 27g
Cholesterol: 0g	Protein: 4g

Add blackberries, raspberries, and honey to a large saucepan; cover, and cook on medium low until berries are thawed. Combine lemon juice and cornstarch; add to the berries, and gently stir. Evenly spoon into lightly oiled individual ramekins. (May use an 8x8-inch cake pan instead of ramekins.)

TOPPING:

1 cup white whole-wheat flour

½ teaspoon sea salt

½ teaspoon cinnamon

¼ cup canola oil

2 tablespoons honey

Preheat oven to 350°.

In a medium mixing bowl, whisk together flour, salt, and cinnamon. Add canola oil, and stir to combine. Lastly, add honey; use hands to combine mixture into crumbs. Sprinkle crumbs over mini cobblers. Bake on a cookie sheet lined with parchment paper; loosely cover with foil after 10 minutes. Bake an additional 10–15 minutes, until tops are golden and juice is hot and bubbly.

Ganache-Covered Strawberries

Ganache-Covered Strawberries

YIELD: 10 SERVINGS   SERVING SIZE: 2 STRAWBERRIES

This recipe is so beautiful, you'd never guess it takes only minutes to prepare. Strawberries are a great source of vitamins C and E, and have been shown to be an anti-arthritic food.

1 cup dark chocolate chips

1 tablespoon coconut oil

20 whole strawberries with leaves, rinsed and dried (1 pound)

Dried coconut flakes or minced almonds for garnish (optional)

NUTRITIONAL DATA
Calories: 139
Total Fat: 10g
Saturated Fat: 6g
Trans Fat: 0g
Cholesterol: 0mg
Sodium: 8mg
Carbohydrates: 14g
Dietary Fiber: 2g
Sugars: 10g
Protein: 2g

Add ½ cup water to bottom of double boiler, and bring to a simmer over medium-low heat. Add chocolate chips and coconut oil to top boiler, and stir until smooth and completely melted. Remove chocolate from heat, and set aside.

Line a 15x10x1-inch cookie sheet with parchment paper. While holding strawberries by the leaves, dip into the chocolate until all but the last ½ inch near the leaf is covered; lift and twist, allowing excess chocolate to drip off. Set strawberries on parchment paper until all strawberries are covered.

For an extra-special treat, immediately after excess chocolate drips from each strawberry, roll in dried coconut flakes or minced almonds.

The chocolate should set in 25–30 minutes.

Chocolate Peanut Butter Almond Bars

YIELD: 6 SERVINGS   SERVING SIZE: 1 BAR

Why have a processed candy bar when you can have a superfoods, all-natural yummy bar? This bar is chock-full of antioxidant flavonoids and dietary fiber, and is low in cholesterol and sodium. Plenty of protein is also a big reason to munch down on these anytime bars.

½ cup oats
20 whole dates, pitted
⅓ cup plus 1 tablespoon natural extra crunchy peanut butter
1 tablespoon wheat germ
¼ cup almonds, with skins
¼ cup bittersweet chocolate chips

NUTRITIONAL DATA

Calories: 376	Sodium: 3g
Total Fat: 13g	Carbohydrates: 63g
Saturated Fat: 3g	Dietary Fiber: 10g
Trans Fat: 0g	Sugars: 33g
Cholesterol: 0g	Protein: 10g

Preheat oven to 325°.

Line a cookie sheet with parchment paper, and evenly distribute oats. Toast until lightly golden, about 20 minutes. Allow to cool at room temperature.

Add dates to a food processor; pulse until dates are one big glob. (It's very important to make sure the dates are more than just diced, but are as stated, "one big glob.") Add peanut butter; pulse until combined. Add toasted oats and wheat germ with almonds, and continue to pulse until all ingredients are well combined. Scrape sides, and pulse one additional time.

Add dough to a mixing bowl. Dough will be a little sticky; if necessary, add one drop of water to make it easier to handle. Use the same lined cookie sheet as above. Shape dough into 3x1-inch bars, using ¼ cup to measure. Place bars on cookie sheet.

In a small saucepan, add chocolate chips; melt over low heat, stirring continuously. Remove from heat, and spread across the tops of bars. Allow chocolate to cool; place bars in an airtight container; and refrigerate until ready to eat. Refrigerating will help take away the stickiness.

Fudge Yum Yums

YIELD: 7½ SERVINGS   SERVING SIZE: 2 YUM YUMS

I've re-created these childhood candies and turned them into a chocolate lover's superfood dream. These candies are low in sodium and cholesterol and high in protein.

2 cups dark chocolate chips (SunSpire Grain Sweetened Dark Chocolate Baking Chips were used)

¼ cup honey

½ cup lite coconut milk, canned

1 teaspoon vanilla extract

½ cup natural crunchy peanut butter, no sugar added

3 cups old-fashioned oats

NUTRITIONAL DATA	
Calories: 361	Sodium: 6g
Total Fat: 16g	Carbohydrates: 48g
Saturated Fat: 6g	Dietary Fiber: 7g
Trans Fat: 0g	Sugars: 14g
Cholesterol: 1g	Protein: 9g

In a large heavy saucepan, combine chocolate chips, honey, and coconut milk. On low heat, allow chocolate mixture to melt while stirring every few minutes. When chocolate mixture is completely melted, remove from heat. Add vanilla and peanut butter; stir to combine. Fold oats into mixture, and stir to coat. Using a tablespoon, drop cookies onto a piece of wax paper or parchment paper. Allow to cool completely before placing in a container with lid.

Note: Yum Yums will continue to get firm after being refrigerated. Refrigerate for up to three days.

Dark Chocolate Nut Clusters

YIELD: 12 SERVINGS   **SERVING SIZE: 2 CLUSTERS**

Dark chocolate is rich in flavonoids, which may help in lowering blood pressure and improving blood flow to the brain and heart. Enjoy this treat, and get a beneficial amount of vitamin E, copper, and manganese.

1 cup roasted raw almonds, with skins

1 cup roasted raw pistachios

½ cup dark chocolate chips (SunSpire Grain Sweetened Dark Chocolate Baking Chips were used)

½ teaspoon sea salt (Fleur de Sel recommended)

NUTRITIONAL DATA	
Calories: 106	Sodium: 48mg
Total Fat: 9g	Carbohydrates: 5g
Saturated Fat: 1g	Dietary Fiber: 2g
Trans Fat: 0g	Sugars: 1g
Cholesterol: 0mg	Protein: 4g

Preheat oven to 325°.

Line a rimmed cookie sheet with parchment paper; evenly spread almonds and pistachios onto sheet. Roast 12 minutes. Cool at room temperature.

In a medium saucepan, combine chocolate and salt; melt over low heat, while stirring, until completely melted, 3–4 minutes. Add almonds and pistachios to chocolate; toss to cover. Pour chocolate-covered nuts onto the same lined cookie sheet; spread flat, but keep nuts next to each other in order to form 1 piece.

Allow to cool at room temperature; refrigerate 30 minutes if chocolate is still sticky. Break into 1- to 2-inch pieces. Store in an airtight container for up to 3 days.

Tip: If the temperature is warm outside, store in the refrigerator.

Benefits and Sources of Vitamins

With very few exceptions the human body cannot manufacture or synthesize vitamins. They must be supplied in our diet or in man-made dietary supplements. Some people believe that supplements can replace food, but that is incorrect. In fact, vitamins cannot be assimilated without also ingesting food. That's why it is best to take them with a meal.

Note: We have listed only those superfoods contained in this cookbook that contain significant quantities of these vitamins.

VITAMIN	SOURCES
Vitamin A (Alpha-carotene, beta-carotene, and retinol) Helps cell reproduction. It also stimulates immunity and is needed for formation of some hormones. Helps vision and promotes bone growth, tooth development, and helps maintain healthy skin, hair, and mucous membranes. Effective preventive against measles.	Bok Choy, Broccoli, Brussels Sprouts, Carrots, Eggs, Grapefruit, Green Peas, Kale, Mangoes, Napa Cabbage, Pecans, Pistachios, Spinach, Squash, Sweet Potatoes, Swiss Chard, Tomatoes
Vitamin B1 (Thiamine) Helps the body cells convert carbohydrates into energy. It is also essential for the functioning of the heart, muscles, and nervous system. Not getting enough thiamine can leave one fatigued and weak.	Asparagus, Avocados, Beans (most), Brussels Sprouts, Dates, Flax Seeds, Grapefruit, Green Peas, Mangoes, Oats, Oranges, Pecans, Pine Nuts, Pineapple, Pistachios, Quinoa, Rice (brown), Salmon, Sweet Potatoes, Yogurt
Vitamin B2 (Riboflavin) Important for body growth, reproduction, and red cell production. It also helps in releasing energy from carbohydrates.	Almonds, Artichokes, Asparagus, Avocados, Bananas, Beans (most), Bok Choy, Brussels Sprouts, Dates, Eggs, Green Peas, Mangoes, Mushrooms, Oats, Quinoa, Salmon, Sweet Potatoes, Swiss Chard, Yogurt
Vitamin B3 (Niacin) Assists in the functioning of the digestive system, skin, and nerves. It is also important for the conversion of food to energy.	Artichokes, Avocados, Beans (most), Dates, Green Peas, Mangoes, Mushrooms, Salmon, Squash, Sweet Potatoes
Vitamin B5 Essential for the metabolism of food as well as in the formation of hormones and (good) cholesterol.	Avocados, Beans (some), Broccoli, Brussels Sprouts, Dates, Eggs, Grapefruit, Mushrooms, Oats, Raspberries, Salmon, Squash, Sweet Potatoes, Yogurt
Vitamin B6 Plays a role in the creation of antibodies in the immune system. Helps maintain normal nerve function and acts in the formation of red blood cells. It is also required for the chemical reactions of proteins. Too little B6 in the diet can cause dizziness, nausea, confusion, irritability, and convulsions.	Avocados, Bananas, Beans (most), Bok Choy, Broccoli, Brussels Sprouts, Chestnuts, Dates, Green Peas, Kale, Mangoes, Pineapple, Pistachios, Pumpkin Seeds, Rice (brown), Salmon, Squash, Sweet Potatoes, Walnuts
Vitamin B9 (Folate and folic acid) Folate occurs naturally in fresh foods; folic acid is the synthetic form found in supplements. Your body needs folate to produce red blood cells, and components of the nervous system. It helps in maintaining normal brain function, and is a critical part of spinal fluid. Folic acid is vital for proper cell growth, and development of the embryo during pregnancy.	Artichokes, Asparagus, Avocados, Beetroot, Blackberries, Bok Choy, Broccoli, Brussels Sprouts, Dates, Green Peas, Mangoes, Napa Cabbage, Oranges, Pineapple, Raspberries, Spinach, Squash, Strawberries
Vitmain B12 Like the other B vitamins, vitamin B12 is important for metabolism. It helps in the formation of red blood cells and in the maintenance of the central nervous system.	Vitamin B12 is the one vitamin that is available only from fish, poultry, meat, or dairy sources. Eggs, Salmon, Yogurt
Vitamin C Plays a significant role as an antioxidant, protecting body tissue from the damage of oxidation. Antioxidants protect cells against the effects of free radicals. Free radicals can cause cell damage that may contribute to the development of cardiovascular disease and cancer. Also an effective antiviral agent.	Bok Choy, Broccoli, Brussels Sprouts, Grapefruit, Kale, Kiwi, Mangoes, Oranges, Pineapple, Strawberries, Squash (some), Swiss Chard, Yogurt
Vitamin D Manufactured by the body after being exposed to sunshine. Ten to fifteen minutes of good sunshine three times weekly is adequate to produce the body's requirement of vitamin D. This means that we don't need to obtain vitamin D from our diet unless we get very little sunlight—usually not a problem for children. Vitamin D is vital to the human body as it promotes absorption of calcium and magnesium, which are essential for the normal development of healthy teeth and bones.	Eggs, Mushrooms, Yogurt
Vitamin E Like vitamin C, it plays a significant role as an antioxidant. Important in the formation of red blood cells, and the use of vitamin K. Also used topically to help minimize the appearance of wrinkles, and heal minor wounds without scarring.	Almonds, Avocados, Blackberries, Blueberries, Cranberries, Eggs, Kiwi, Mangoes, Pine Nuts, Pinto Beans, Raspberries, Squash (some), Swiss Chard
Vitamin K Fat soluble and plays a critical role in blood clotting. It regulates blood calcium levels, and activates at least three proteins involved in bone health.	Artichokes, Asparagus, Avocados, Berries (most), Bok Choy, Broccoli, Brussels Sprouts, Cabbage, Carrots, Cauliflower, Eggs, Green Peas, Kale, Kidney Beans, Kiwi, Mangoes, Pine Nuts, Pistachios, Pomegranate, Spinach, Squash (some), Swiss Chard, Tomatoes

Suggested Health Benefits of Superfoods

In order for a food to be labeled a superfood, it must offer health benefits above and beyond its normal nutritional value. Scientists believe these foods may help fight and protect against many illnesses, some of which are listed here.

Almonds	Strengthen bones	Combat cancer	Guard against heart disease	Lower cholesterol	Reduce the risk of heart attacks
Artichokes	Aid in digestion	Lower cholesterol	Protect your heart	Stabilize blood sugar	Guard against liver disease
Apples	Protect your heart	Prevent constipation	Combat cancer	Improve lung capacity	Cushion joints
Asparagus	Regulates blood sugar	Promotes weight loss	Promotes healthy immune system	Is a natural diuretic	Aids in cardiovascular function
Avocados	Battle diabetes	Lower cholesterol	Stabilize your eyesight	Protect your heart	Slow aging process
Bananas	Protect your heart	Quiet a cough	Strengthen bones	Control high blood pressure	Block diarrhea
Beans	Lower cholesterol	Combat cancer	Prevent constipation	Stabilize blood sugar	Help hemorrhoids
Beets	Control blood pressure	Combat cancer	Strengthen bones	Protect your heart	Promote weight loss
Bell Peppers	Lower cholesterol	Combat colon cancer	Promote weight loss	Decrease the risk of strokes	Protect your heart
Berries (general)	Combat cancer	Slow aging process	Combat heart disease	Protect your heart	Prevent constipation
Blueberries	Combat cancer	Prevent constipation	Stabilize blood sugar	Protect your heart	Boost memory
Broccoli	Strengthens bones	Saves eyesight	Combats cancer	Protects your heart	Controls blood pressure
Brown Rice	Battles diabetes	Conquers kidney stones	Combats cancer	Protects your heart	Decreases the risk of strokes
Brussels Sprouts	Combat cancer	Promote weight loss	Reduce chronic inflammation	Reduce cholesterol	Combat oxidative stress
Cabbage	Prevents constipation	Promotes weight loss	Combats cancer	Protects your heart	Helps hemorrhoids
Carrots	Save eyesight	Prevent constipation	Combat cancer	Protect your heart	Promote weight loss
Cauliflower	Strengthens bones	Banishes Bruises	Combats breast cancer	Protects against prostate cancer	Guards against heart disease
Chard	Promotes weight loss	Lowers cholesterol	Boosts immune system	Strengthens bones	Protects against colon and prostate cancer
Cherries	Combat cancer	Slow aging process	Combat insomnia	Protect your heart	Shield against Alzheimer's
Coconut (oil, flakes, and water)	Increases energy	Boosts metabolism	Promotes weight loss	Kills bacteria	Fights fungus
Dark Chocolate	Controls blood pressure	Decreases the risk of strokes	Regulates blood sugar	Boosts moods	Combats cancer
Dates	Prevent constipation	Prevent abdominal cancer	Control your appetite	Maintain heart health	Prevents intestinal disorders
Eggs	Combat breast cancer	Save eyesight	Control your appetite	Promote heart health	Aid in muscle repair
Fennel	Combats anemia	Facilitates digestion	Regulates menstruation	Combats flatulence	Prevents constipation
Flax seeds	Aid in digestion	Battle diabetes	Protect your heart	Improve mental health	Boost immune system
Garlic	Lowers cholesterol	Controls blood pressure	Combats cancer	Kills bacteria	Fights fungus
Grapefruit	Protects against heart attacks	Promotes weight loss	Helps stop strokes	Combats prostate cancer	Lowers cholesterol

(continued on next page)

Suggested Health Benefits of Superfoods (continued)

Green Peas	Lower cholesterol	Boost immune system	Strengthen bones	Support immune system	Combat lung cancer
Green Tea	Protects your heart	Promotes weight loss	Helps stop strokes	Combats cancer	Kills bacteria
Hazelnuts	Prevent cataracts	Improve circulation	Relieve allergies	Control blood pressure	Combat cancer
Honey	Heals wounds	Aids in digestion	Guards against ulcers	Increases energy	Fights allergies
Kale	Combats cancer	Protects your heart	Prevents cataracts	Prevents osteoporosis	Shields against arthritis
Kiwi	Lowers cholesterol	Promotes respiratory health	Improves vision	Combats colon cancer	Prevents asthma
Legumes	Prevent food cravings	Combat cancer	Boost energy	Stabilize blood sugar	Protect against diabetes
Lemons	Protect your heart	Control blood pressure	Smooth your skin	Combat cancer	Stop scurvy
Mangoes	Boost memory	Regulate your thyroid	Aid in digestion	Combat cancer	Shield against Alzheimer's
Mushrooms	Control blood pressure	Kill bacteria	Strengthen bones	Combat cancer	Lower cholesterol
Nuts in general	Protect against heart disease	Lower cholesterol	Prevent food cravings	Boost immune system	Prevent constipation
Oats	Battle diabetes	Prevent constipation	Smooth your skin	Combat cancer	Lower cholesterol
Onions	Reduce risk of heart attacks	Promote weight loss	Help stop strokes	Combat cancer	Lower cholesterol
Oranges	Support immune systems	Combat cancer	Protect your heart	Promote respiratory health	Prevent constipation
Pecans	Control blood pressure	Combat breast cancer	Lower cholesterol	Combat prostate cancer	Promote weight loss
Peanuts	Protect against heart disease	Promote weight loss	Combat prostate cancer	Lower cholesterol	Aggravate diverticulitis
Pine Nuts	Appetite suppressant	Lower cholesterol	Improve circulation	Slow the aging process	Boost energy
Pineapple	Strengthens bones	Relieves colds	Aids in digestion	Dissolves warts	Blocks diarrhea
Pistachios	Lower cholesterol	Boost energy	Combat cancer	Protect against infections	Smoothes skin
Pumpkin Seeds	Promote prostate health	Strengthen bones	Protect against arthritis	Lower cholesterol	Combat cancer
Quinoa	Stabilizes blood sugar	Builds muscle tissue	Prevents constipation	Strengthens bones	Boosts energy
Salmon, Fish	Protect your heart	Boost your memory	Combat cancer	Support immune system	Protect against arthritis
Spinach	Safeguards against blindness	Curbs appetite	Controls blood pressure	Aids in digestion	Combats skin cancer
Squash	Combats lung disease	Protects against emphysema	Protects your heart	Protects against birth defects	Reduces inflammation
Strawberries	Combat cancer	Protect your heart	Boost memory	Calm stress	Reduce inflammation
Sweet Potatoes	Save your eyesight	Boost moods	Combat cancer	Strengthen bones	Maintain skin's elasticity
Tomatoes	Protect your prostate	Combat cancer	Lower cholesterol	Protect your heart	Improve vision
Walnuts	Lower cholesterol	Combat cancer	Boost memory	Boost moods	Protect against heart disease
Yogurt	Guards against ulcers	Strengthens bones	Lowers cholesterol	Supports immune system	Aids in digestion

Note: This chart is not intended to provide medical advice. Always consult a doctor or nutritionist before making any drastic changes to your dietary intake.

Converting Recipes to Metric Measures

These conversions only work with U.S. recipes. Some measurements have been rounded off slightly, but all conversions should be sufficient for all the recipes included in this cookbook.

Volume Conversions
Normally used for liquids, herbs, and spices

U.S. QUANTITY	METRIC
¼ teaspoon	1.25 mL
½ teaspoon	2.5 mL
¾ teaspoon	3.75 mL
1 teaspoon	5 mL
1 tablespoon or ½ fluid ounce	15 mL
1 fluid ounce or ⅛ cup	30 mL
¼ cup or 2 fluid ounces	60 mL
⅓ cup	80 mL
½ cup or 4 fluid ounces	120 mL
⅔ cup	160 mL
¾ cup or 6 fluid ounces	180 mL
1 cup or 8 fluid ounces or ½ pint	240 mL
1¼ cups	300 mL
1⅓ cups	330 mL
1½ cups or 12 fluid ounces	350 mL
1⅔ cups	390 mL
1¾ cups	415 mL
2 cups or 1 pint or 16 fluid ounces	475 mL
2½ cups	600 mL
3 cups or 1½ pints	700 mL
3½ cups	830 mL
4 cups or 2 pints or 1 quart	950 mL
2 quarts or ½ gallon	1.9 L
4 quarts or 1 gallon	3.8 L

KEY:
mL = milliliters   g = grams
L = liters   cm = centimeters
1 L = 1,000 mL   mm = millimeters
  1 cm = 10 mm

Weight Conversions
See Volume Conversions for fluid ounces

U.S. QUANTITY	METRIC
1 ounce	28 g
4 ounces or ¼ pound	113 g
⅓ pound	150 g
8 ounces or ½ pound	230 g
⅔ pound	300 g
12 ounces or ¾ pound	340 g
1 pound or 16 ounces	450 g
2 pounds	900 g

Length Conversions

U.S. QUANTITY	METRIC
⅛ inch	3 mm
¼ inch	6 mm
½ inch	13 mm
¾ inch	19 mm
1 inch	2.5 cm
2 inches	5 cm
3 inches	7.6 cm
4 inches	10 cm
5 inches	13 cm
6 inches	15 cm
7 inches	18 cm
8 inches	20 cm
9 inches	23 cm
10 inches	25 cm
12 inches or 1 foot	30 cm

Index

About the Authors

"It's an attitude not a waist size," say authors Tiffany McCauley and Gale Compton about their philosophy of helping people maintain a healthy weight. They recommend focusing on unprocessed ingredients, from real herbs and spices to fresh veggies and whole grains. The result? Two cookbooks so far: *Skinny Ms. Slow Cooker* (published January 2011) and *Skinny Ms. Superfoods*. Stay tuned to see what's next!

Pamela Photography

Tiffany McCauley

Tiffany McCauley discovered her love for cooking at age eighteen as an au pair in Stuttgart, Germany. She developed a passion for creating delicious recipes from scratch. However, after gaining 114 pounds over a 15-year period, and with the birth of her son, she learned the importance of good health. Her desire and commitment to teach her son proper nutrition inspired her to change her eating habits and take control of her weight.

To date, Tiffany has lost nearly sixty pounds by following the eating style applied to the recipes in this book. In 2011, Tiffany achieved a lifelong goal of running a marathon.

Born and raised in the San Francisco Bay area, Tiffany currently lives in northern California with her husband, a U.S. Marine Corps veteran, and their four-year-old son.

Gale Compton

A little girl growing up in the South is wrapped in a world of tradition. Looking back, Gale Compton ties her love for family and cooking to Sunday afternoons in her grandmother's kitchen.

Gale's early adulthood was marked by a youthful sense of culinary discovery while living for seven years in Germany. There is no question this exposure to other cultures deepened and broadened her love for the culinary arts.

Diagnosed with breast cancer for the second time in less than a year, and facing the fight of her life, Gale knew she had to make powerful changes in her diet and her lifestyle. So her cupboards got clean . . . and so did Gale.

Bonnie Clinton Photography

Today, Gale is a certified fitness trainer, wife, mom, and coauthor.